BIBLE-BELIEVING STUDIES ON

SATAN'S

COUNTERFEITS

Michael D. O'Neal

Printed in the United States of America

O'Neal, Michael D. 1953 -
Bible-Believing Studies in Revelation / Michael D. O'Neal
ISBN 13: 978-0-578-91481-7 (Hardcover)
ISBN 10: 0-578-91481-6

All Scripture quotations are taken from the Holy Bible, King James Version

BIBLE-BELIEVING STUDIES ON

SATAN'S

COUNTERFEITS

Michael D. O'Neal

TABLE OF CONTENTS

ACKNOWLEDGEMENTS

I want to thank my wife, Jane, for her help in encouragement and in proofreading; missionary Danny Jones for formatting the book and giving counsel about publishing; Bill Goins for his awesome cover design; and James Bowe and others for proofreading.

Everything that I do is dedicated to the glory of my Lord and Savior Jesus Christ. Additionally, I would like to dedicate this book to our daughters, Grace and Joy, for the happiness that they have brought to their mother and me.

INTRODUCTION

TO BE "LIKE THE MOST HIGH"

I'm assuming that the type of person who would be reading this book already believes in the reality and personality of the devil.

However, how much do you really know about the devil? If you do believe that he is real, have you seen him lately? Have you recognized his devices that he uses against you so that you are aware of how to be able to resist him? You do understand that he is your adversary, right? The Bible says in:

1 Peter 5:8 Be sober, be vigilant; because your adversary the devil, as a roaring lion, walketh about, seeking whom he may devour:

Then the next verse gives a command:

1 Peter 5:9 Whom resist stedfast in the faith, knowing that the same afflictions are accomplished in your brethren that are in the world.

So the Bible commands us to resist the devil. That brings up a question to you, my Christian friend. By the way, if you are NOT a Christian, you are already in the clutches of the devil whether or not you believe it. You are powerless to resist him until you truly know the God of heaven and the Lord Jesus Christ as your Savior. If you are not 100 percent certain that you are saved, I urge you to turn to Christ in faith, trusting Him and His payment for your sins with His own blood on the cross of Calvary!

Now, as I was saying, the command to resist the devil brings up a question for the Christian. That question is: How are you going to resist the devil if you are ignorant about him? The Bible says in:

2 Corinthians 2:11 Lest Satan should get an advantage of us: for we are not ignorant of his devices.

If you're saved, you have the power in you to defeat the devil. That power in you is the Lord Himself! If you are saved, the Lord is in you! And the Bible says in:

> **1 John 4:4 Ye are of God, little children, and have overcome them: because greater is he that is in you, than he that is in the world.**

Why is it, then, that the devil has been able to defeat you so many times? Perhaps it is because you are, to some degree, "IGNORANT of his devices."

In this book we are going to "give the devil his due." In so doing, we are likely to find him resisting our efforts. It wouldn't surprise me if I face a lot of opposition in completing the writing of this manuscript. It wouldn't surprise me if you face opposition in completing the reading of this book.

I've been preaching for many years. A few times when I have preached about the devil some strange things have happened.

In my first pastorate, a light ballast started going bad while I was preaching a sermon on the devil. I didn't realize what was going on, but wires in the ballast started melting, and the smell of the burning began to permeate the auditorium. Now THAT was a special effect! People started sniffing and smelling smoke while I was in the pulpit preaching hellfire and brimstone! You have heard of sound effects. These were SMELL effects! One of our church men finally got up and hunted down the odor. Sure enough, we had a ballast that had some melting wires.

It would be nice if we could smell the devil every time that he walked near us, wouldn't it? I'm sorry to inform you of this, but the roaring lion of 1 Pet. 5:8 doesn't smell like he's on fire. He smells like the environment that he is in, and one of his main environments for doing his work is the local church. I believe that two of the devil's main arenas of attack are religion and education. Also, Satan doesn't always roar when he is a good distance away in stalking his prey. If he did that, you would have time to flee. When Satan roars, it is usually too late!

I want us to introduce our studies by reading an Old Testament passage that reveals the truth about the devil's great desire:

TO BE LIKE THE MOST HIGH

I'm sure that there are a number of things that Satan desires. In Luke 22:31 Jesus said that Satan desired Peter, that he might sift him as wheat. But we are going to concentrate on the desire of the devil that is expressed in the following passage:

> **Isaiah 14:12-15 How art thou fallen from heaven, O Lucifer, son of the morning! how art thou cut down to the ground, which didst weaken the nations! 13 For thou hast said in thine heart, I will ascend into heaven, I will exalt my throne above the stars of God: I will sit also upon the mount of the congregation, in the sides of the north: 14 I will ascend above the heights of the clouds; I will be like the most High. 15 Yet thou shalt be brought down to hell, to the sides of the pit.**

Among the things that Lucifer (another name for the devil, Satan) said that he was going to do is this, "I will be like the most High."

So, there it is. That, I believe, is Satan's great desire: to be LIKE the most High.

If you would like to know the warnings that the Bible gives you about the devil, I'm going to give you some key passages to study. One reason you ought to study them is to enable yourself to better resist the devil. The main reason why I believe you ought to study the devil is to fight him. You want to study him so you can learn his devices and know what he's going to do. That's what 1 Peter 5:8 has in view. You can recognize what Satan is doing if you know what the word of God says. God does not want His children to be ignorant of the Devil's wiles:

> **2 Corinthians 2:11 Lest Satan should get an advantage of us: for we are not ignorant of his devices.**

That's why those passages are in the Bible, my friend. They are there to warn you, not to glorify the devil. If all of the Bible was written to glorify the personality of the narrative, you wouldn't find anything in the Bible except scriptures about God. So the things written in the Bible about the devil are not written to praise him but to warn you. When I write these words about the devil, I have no joy at all in the subject matter. I do not want to give Satan undue attention in the sense of adoration or praise. I just desire to expose him as the dangerous, wicked creature that he is. I do want to warn you, because he is real, and he is after you.

Those key passages in the word of God that reveal a lot about our adversary, the devil, are Genesis 3, Job 1, 2, 41, Isaiah 14, Ezekiel 28, Matthew 4, Luke 4, 2 Corinthians 11, and Revelation 12, 19, 20, and 21. These passages show you many things about the devices, the desire, and, praise God, the defeat and destination of the devil. He's going to end up in the lake of fire, according to Revelation 20.

The passage in Isaiah 14 describes the fall of Lucifer. Prophetically, it refers to his future fall in the tribulation period, when the devil is incarnate as the Man of Sin, the antichrist. It also refers, however, to his fall from heaven some time in ages past.

According to Ezekiel 28, our enemy was once the "anointed cherub which covereth." That is what he is called in Ezekiel 28:14:

> **Ezekiel 28:14 Thou art the anointed cherub that covereth; and I have set thee so: thou wast upon the holy mountain of God; thou hast walked up and down in the midst of the stones of fire.**

Those cherubims, which covered the ark of the testament with their wings in the Old Testament, have their counterparts in heaven at the throne of God. They are described in Revelation 4, where they appear to be four in number. If the devil was once also one of the cherubims and fell, that means there was once a FIFTH cherub, who was Satan himself (and contrary to what most Bible numerics lessons teach, the number five is often OMINOUSLY significant, having nothing to do whatsoever with the most frequently assumed theme of grace, but rather with the theme of DEATH, and its predecessor, PRIDE. Please note the five occurrences of "I" in Isa. 14:12-14 about Lucifer; in Isa. 10:12-14 about the Assyrian, the antichrist; in Lk. 18:10-12 about the Pharisee; and the five occurrences of "us" in Gen. 11:1-4 about the builders of the tower of Babel).

According to the description given in the book of Ezekiel, Lucifer is a musical creature. Watch out, pastors, for church treasurers (Judas Iscariot was a treasurer), and watch out for song leaders (Satan may have been heaven's song leader).

Why is it that Lucifer fell? The Bible says he was perfect in all his ways since the day he was created, until iniquity was found in him (Ezek. 28:15). What was it that caused him to fall? Undoubtedly, it was PRIDE. In 1 Tim. 3:6 pride is said to be the condemnation of the devil. In giving the qualifications of a bishop, the Bible says in:

1 Timothy 3:6 Not a novice, lest being lifted up with pride he fall into the condemnation of the devil.

According to the above verse, the condemnation of the devil was his pride. Five times in Isa. 14 he said, "I will." One of those ambitions was to be "like the most High."

I want to stir you in these chapters, but I also want you to receive, to think, and to learn from this material. I want you to give the matter some time for consideration, looking these things up in the word of God to see if they are the truth. The word of God says of the Bereans in:

Acts 17:11 These were more noble than those in Thessalonica, in that they received the word with all readiness of mind, and searched the scriptures daily, whether those things were so.

Now pay attention. A common proclamation from the average pulpit is that the Christian's goal should be to "be like Jesus." Someone might conclude that from reading passages of scripture which tell us that God wants us to be godly. However, I want you to think about the fact that in the King James Bible nobody filled with the Spirit of God ever said, "I want to be LIKE the most High." Think about that. Nobody in the scriptures who was filled with God's Spirit ever said, "I want to be LIKE God." Nobody who was right with God said, "I would be LIKE Jesus." A song writer may have said that, but the SCRIPTURES didn't.

Did you hear me? I said that nobody, NOBODY in the word of God, who was filled with the Spirit of God, ever said, "I want to be LIKE Christ," or "I want to be LIKE Jesus." It may shock you to discover that in the Bible only the DEVIL himself is recorded as wanting to be like God! That's right! In the scriptures, only the devil himself wanted to be LIKE Christ. In the word of God, only the DEVIL is recorded as trying to be LIKE the Lord!

Sometimes Christians, because of their association with the Lord, their obedience to Him, and their following of him, are thought of by others as being LIKE the Lord, but that is GOD'S doing. Being like God in that sense is just a by-product of your believing God, obeying God, following God, and listening to God, but not of your IMITATING God. Notice that Paul commended the Thessalonian believers for being FOLLOWERS:

1 Thessalonians 1:6 And ye became followers of us, and of the Lord, having received the word in much affliction, with joy of the Holy Ghost:

The new "bibles," in places where they should refer to people as FOLLOWERS of the Lord, such as 1 Thess. 1:6 above, in nearly every case use the word "IMITATORS." Now, friend, an imitation is a phony. There is a lot of difference between FOLLOWING the Lord and IMITATING Him. An imitator is someone who tries to "pass himself off" as someone else. For example, if you go to a restaurant and try to pay for your meal with imitation currency, don't be surprised if you get a negative reaction from the cashier.

Do you know why those "bibles" (and I use the term loosely) use the word "imitators" instead of "followers"? It's because they are IMITATION Bibles. They are not the real thing; they are imitations! I'll examine this fact in some detail in Chapter Five, "Imitation Scriptures."

The main desire of Satan is not to legalize abortion, although he was probably involved in the Supreme Court's abominable decision to accomplish that. The main desire of the devil is not to remove firearms from the hands of American citizens. His main desire is not to ban prayer in the public schools, although he probably had a hand in that. The MAIN desire of Satan, I believe, is TO BE LIKE GOD. That is his great motivation. That is one of the things that keeps him going -- to be like God.

Some time in ages long past, the devil sinned by declaring, "I will be like the most High." Rather than ascend above the stars of God as he aspired, however, he fell. At an unspecified later date, he showed up on the earth in a perfect environment, the Garden of Eden. The devil spoke to the woman (gentlemen, take note, because this is a common practice of his). In his efforts to get her to eat the forbidden fruit, he told her that if she and Adam ate of it, they would be AS GODS, knowing good and evil. Satan said in:

> **Genesis 3:5 For God doth know that in the day ye eat thereof, then your eyes shall be opened, and ye shall be as gods, knowing good and evil.**

Pay attention now. I'm telling you that in the Bible we find that Satan wants to be LIKE GOD.

We who are saved are going to be conformed to the image of God's Son some day at the Rapture. At that time, the Bible says, we shall be LIKE Him.

> **1 John 3:2 Beloved, now are we the sons of God, and it doth not yet appear what we shall be: but we know that, when he shall appear, we shall be like him; for we shall see him as he is.**

Until that time, you should FOLLOW the Lord. It is even scriptural for you to follow PEOPLE who are following the Lord. The Bible says in:

1 Corinthians 11:1 Be ye followers of me, even as I also am of Christ.

1 Thessalonians 2:14 For ye, brethren, became followers of the churches of God which in Judaea are in Christ Jesus: for ye also have suffered like things of your own countrymen, even as they have of the Jews:

Until the Rapture, take the Bible and read it, heed it, memorize it, meditate on it, do your best to live by it, and, as a by-product, you WILL be somewhat like the Lord. However, this will be a by-product of OBEYING the Lord, NOT of a desire or scheme on your part to IMITATE Him. You should just endeavor to be what you ought to be for God. Don't TRY to be God. Don't TRY to be anybody ELSE. Just be who GOD wants you to be! Don't try to be LIKE God. Don't try to be LIKE Jesus. Don't try to be LIKE your favorite preacher. Don't try to be like ANYBODY! Just endeavor to obey God. Follow the Lord, and follow those who are following Him.

If someone else is obeying God, get right behind him and do what he does.

Philippians 4:9 Those things, which ye have both learned, and received, and heard, and seen in me, do: and the God of peace shall be with you.

But don't do it in an effort to pass yourself off as that person. That is what imitating is really all about. Someone says, "My goal in life is to be like the Lord," and those listening say, "That is a wonderful goal." Is that so? THE DEVIL had that goal, and he got kicked out of his position.

I want you to examine with me this desire of Satan. I believe that if we are observant, we will recognize his handiwork in the hearts and lives of men today, including ourselves. Sometimes Christian people seem to think that they are immune to the devil's work. That's not so. You're only immune to the devil's work to the extent that God sees fit to protect you at any given time. If you are not sober and vigilant (1 Pet. 5:8), if you are not prayerful, if you do not resist Satan, the Lord will remove the hedge of protection (Job 1:10) and allow Satan to teach you a lesson.

Just try defeating Satan in your own strength and see how far you get. Say, "I'm mature enough as a Christian now to handle things on my own. I'm going to quit reading my Bible. I know enough." You'll see. You'll "go down the tubes." You say, "I'm spiritual enough now. I think I'll just quit going soul-winning." You watch. Your spirituality will go down the toilet. Say, "I'm old in the Lord. I don't have to tithe anymore." Give it a shot then, buddy. God will allow the devil to "beat the devil" out of you. You'll be asking yourself, "How did I ever get in this mess?" I'll tell you how you got into the mess: you overestimated yourself and you underestimated your enemy.

I give you the verse again:

> **1 Peter 5:8   Be sober, be vigilant; because your adversary the devil, as a roaring lion, walketh about, seeking whom he may devour:**

In this book we want to see areas in which Satan has intentionally copied the things of God. I'm going to warn you of his efforts to imitate the Lord. But first, I want you to think with me about four appeals or attractions that move Satan to be like the most High. Before we expose the devil's efforts to counterfeit God and the things of God, in this introduction we'll see his motivation for doing that. What caused Satan to desire to be "like the most high?" Look with me at four things that appealed to him, and you'll know something about what has motivated Satan to produce all of these counterfeits of the things of the Lord.

THERE IS THE APPEAL OF ALTITUDE

First, there is the appeal of altitude. Satan said, "I will be like the most HIGH." The appeal of altitude is the desire to "get up in this world," as some people might say it today. It is a desire to excel so much that our achievement can be described as being "out of this world."

Looking again at Isaiah 14, we see that Lucifer said, "I will ASCEND" (that's UP) "into HEAVEN," (that's UP) "I will EXALT" (that's UP) "my throne ABOVE" (that's UP) "the stars" (that's UP) "of God:" (that's UP) "I will sit also upon the MOUNT" (that's UP) "of the congregation, in the sides of the NORTH:" (that's UP) "I will ASCEND" (that's UP) "ABOVE" (that's UP) "the HEIGHTS" (that's UP) "of the CLOUDS;" (that's up) "I will be like the most HIGH" (that's UP) (Isa. 14:12-14). Superman (a type of the antichrist) used to say, "Up, up, and AWAY!"

My friend, would you look at that? How many times does God have to mention something before you and I will take notice? The appeal of getting "up" in this world, of getting above others, is what caused Satan to fall.

The appeal of altitude is the appeal TO HAVE MORE MAJESTY THAN OTHERS. I remember how we, as little children, would occupy ourselves after school with simple games. One of them was called "King of the Hill" or "King of the Mountain." Did you play that? Probably. You may have played King of the Hill 50 years ago, and your children and grandchildren play the same game today. Why don't we play "King of the PIT"? Why don't we play a game in which the object of the game is to get as far down in a hole as you can get? Nobody plays that. Nobody is considered successful if his finances, ambitions, or anything else, go down in the hole.

I read a motivational book once by Zig Ziglar called, "See You at the Top." I have never seen a motivational book titled, "See You at the Bottom." Why is that? Don't Christians know that the best way to get to the top in God's will in honor is to first go down to the bottom in humility?

There is an appeal of altitude, an appeal to have more majesty than others. I believe this is probably connected with what the Bible calls in the book of Revelation the doctrine of the Nicolaitanes (Rev. 2:15).

The appeal of altitude includes the appeal TO HAVE MORE MONEY THAN OTHERS. The Bible says,

> **1 Timothy 6:10 For the love of money is the root of all evil: which while some coveted after, they have erred from the faith, and pierced themselves through with many sorrows.**

The love of money, not money itself, is the root of all evil. What is "the love of money?" The love of money is just the desire to have more than what God wants you to have. It is GREED. That's all. That is why the love of money is the root of ALL evil. It was the root of Satan's fall before money, as we know it, existed.

I understand that money is a necessity of life. As a matter of fact, God has told us in His word how to get money. But we're not supposed to labor to be RICH, and we are not supposed to LOVE money. There is something that infects the heart of a person, so that he gets to CRAVING money. This person HAS to have more money, and he cannot be satisfied unless he has more money than other people. He can't be content to have the same amount as everyone else.

I am not a socialist. I don't think that the government should equalize everyone's income. But some folks just cannot be content to have only as much as what other people have or to have less than what some other people have. They have a hunger to have more money than their friends, their neighbors, and their relatives. That desire, that hunger, is not just worldly. It's not just a lust of the flesh. It's Satanic.

> **Proverbs 23:4   Labour not to be rich: cease from thine own wisdom.**

If you work hard, God will bless your labor.

> **Proverbs 14:23 In all labour there is profit: but the talk of the lips tendeth only to penury.**

There is a danger, however, in the laboring, that we become trapped in a coveting for more financial prosperity than what is due us.

The appeal of altitude is TO HAVE MORE MIGHT THAN OTHERS. The devil wanted to exalt his THRONE, an emblem of power. Some individuals don't feel that they are successful unless they can achieve more power than the common man. American believers get caught in the climbing of the "ladder of success." If you watch cable TV late at night, you will see program after program designed to encourage folks to achieve more majesty, more money, and more might than others. Some of the richest people in America are not just those who have learned to make money by labor; they are people who have learned how to talk people into giving them money by promising to teach those people how to become successful.

Secondly, in the appeal to be like the most High:

THERE IS THE APPEAL OF AWARENESS

By the appeal of awareness, I mean the appeal to have a special degree of knowledge. When the devil spoke to the woman in the garden, he said,

> **Genesis 3:5 For God doth know that in the day ye eat thereof, then your eyes shall be opened, and ye shall be as gods, knowing good and evil.**

This appeal is for **AN EXCEPTIONAL AWARENESS**, to have more knowledge than other people. Friend, be careful about lusting after knowledge. Be circumspect about coveting education. You should even be cautious about desiring wisdom. The gods of this world include education, certification, and accreditation. You need to be sure that you get GOD'S wisdom, and that you get it for HIS honor and glory, to do HIS WILL.

It seems everyone wants a degree after his name. I like the fellow who said he had the B.A. and D.D. degrees. He said they stood for "Born Again Devil Dodger." Well, amen! Someone suggested that for all the good it does sometimes, Ph.D. could just as well stand for Post Hole Digger. A friend of mine said it stood for Permanent Head Damage. I like that one.

I believe a person ought to get all of the training GOD would have him to get, in order to serve in the capacity GOD has for him. You need to prepare for what GOD wants you to be, but that is all. You need to find out what God wants for your life, and get the training required to fulfill God's purpose. Don't pull any of the world's tricks or shortcuts. Just go God's way.

The woman saw that the tree was good for food, that it was pleasant to the eyes, and that it was a tree to be desired TO MAKE ONE WISE. Satan's appeal to the woman was that her increased wisdom would make her and Adam "as gods." Eve succumbed, took of the fruit, ate of it, gave it to her husband, he ate of it, and mankind has never been the same since.

This appeal is for **AN EXTRATERRESTRIAL AWARENESS**, a wisdom possessed by the "gods," not by normal, everyday human beings. That appeal for extraterrestrial awareness, that extraterrestrial wisdom that does not recognize the God of heaven and earth, is of the devil. I am not referring, of course, to your desire to learn from the Lord through legitimate means, such as prayerful study of the scriptures.

What a superstitious country this is in which we live, for us to be as civilized, educated, and technologically advanced as we claim! Here we are in the age of computers, doing things in seconds that took our grandparents hours, days, or weeks. Yet we are still spending money on "spiritual advisors" to learn hidden secrets about our future! I'm not kidding! You say, "Preacher, that's just done in fun." Is that so? Then why do you read your horoscope EVERY DAY? Admit it! You're HOOKED on seeking AN EXTRATERRESTRIAL AWARENESS.

Eric Von Daniken wrote a series of books about gods from outer space. Some of you have read them. I think the first one was called Chariots of the Gods. Von Daniken believed that the earth had received visitors from outer space throughout mankind's history. It was evident to him that these extraterrestrial visitors had taken an active part in the affairs of men, giving supernatural assistance and advice.

Von Daniken was probably right. He just didn't know what to conclude from his observations. There is a spiritual movement today, gearing the minds of the populace to receive answers to the problems of society from outer space. This is old as events in the Bible:

> **Acts 14:11-12 And when the people saw what Paul had done, they lifted up their voices, saying in the speech of Lycaonia, The gods are come down to us in the likeness of men. 12 And they called Barnabas, Jupiter; and Paul, Mercurius, because he was the chief speaker.**

> **Acts 19:35 And when the townclerk had appeased the people, he said, Ye men of Ephesus, what man is there that knoweth not how that the city of the Ephesians is a worshipper of the great goddess Diana, and of the image which fell down from Jupiter?**

I believe this philosophy is a part of the efforts of Satan to deceive and damn mankind, preparing them to be fooled by the antichrist.

The true answers to the problems of sinners are not going to come from occupants of UFOs from heaven! They are going to come from the Author of this BOOK from heaven!! The answers you need are found in God's book, the Bible. Those are ALL the answers you need! You don't need to make King Saul's mistake of seeking an extraterrestrial awareness from someone who has a familiar spirit. I'm not saying that all seers are phony. Far from it. I am just saying that all such endeavors are Satanic.

This appeal is for **AN EXPEDIENT AWARENESS**, that is, something that is the best thing, the most advantageous thing, for you to know at the time. We're talking about "self- help" here. This awareness that Satan wants for himself and offers to those who will listen to him is one that appears to be both appropriate and beneficial. He told the woman that she would know good and evil, as if such extraterrestrial wisdom in such matters is the solution to one's needs. IT IS NOT.

Thirdly, in the desire to be like the most High,

THERE IS THE APPEAL OF ADORATION

The devil wants to be **PRAISED**, like God. He wants to be admired and worshipped. When the devil tempted the Lord Jesus Christ, one of the temptations included the following condition:

> **Matthew 4:8-9 Again, the devil taketh him up into an exceeding high mountain, and sheweth him all the kingdoms of the world, and the glory of them; 9 And saith unto him, All these things will I give thee, if thou wilt fall down and worship me.**

Satan said, after showing the Lord "all the kingdoms of the world, and the glory of them," "All these things I will give thee, if ..." IF? If WHAT? What is the CATCH? -- to get all this stuff? What is the CATCH to get all these kingdoms and their glory? If the devil indeed had the power to give all these things, what was it that he wanted in exchange for such a favor? Answer: "...if thou wilt fall down and worship me." You see, that is the appeal that the devil has, to be like God. He wants the ADORATION that is due God. He wants the PRAISE that is deserved by God.

Satan also wants to be the one to whom **PRAYERS** are addressed. He wants people to fall down before HIM and ask HIM for help and blessings. By the way, there are people who are doing that. Some are doing it knowingly. Additionally, there are those who kneel in prayer, addressing the devil without even knowing it. This even happens in "Christian" churches. There are religious people who disregard the clear teaching of the word of God and at their church's altar call they proceed to the front, where they open their hearts up to just whatever comes along, anything to make them feel as if they have had a spiritual experience. I'll tell you what I believe happens in such cases. I believe unclean spirits move in.

> **1 Corinthians 10:20 But I say, that the things which the Gentiles sacrifice, they sacrifice to devils, and not to God: and I would not that ye should have fellowship with devils.**

The above verse was a warning to BELIEVERS at Corinth! The text indicates that believers might knowingly or unknowingly get in fellowship with the spirits of darkness! Friend, there are devils at work in "worship services."

The devil wants to be PRAISED, he wants to be PRAYED TO, and I believe he also wants to be **PREACHED**, even as God is preached. I believe that as Satan wants to be like the most High, he wants someone to proclaim HIM, Satan. By the way, I am convinced that whenever someone proclaims that salvation is through some other means than through faith in the shed blood of Jesus Christ, he is preaching Satan, even if Satan is not named. You may not understand that, but it is because Satan is often disguised. This brings me to my final point in this introduction:

THERE IS THE APPEAL OF APPEARANCE

The Bible speaks of God's beauty:

> **Psalms 27:4 One thing have I desired of the LORD, that will I seek after; that I may dwell in the house of the LORD all the days of my life, to behold the beauty of the LORD, and to enquire in his temple.**

You see, when people are deceived by the devil, they do not perceive of him as a red character with a long tail and horns (a true depiction, by the way, modified by cartoons). When the devil gets in fellowship with people, he does not introduce himself in his natural clothing of darkness and evil. Rather, he appears angelic. He appears holy. He TRANSFORMS himself into an appealing entity.

> **2 Corinthians 11:14 And no marvel; for Satan himself is transformed into an angel of light.**

Do you really suppose that when the devil made his move on Eve, he slithered up to her, fangs open, venom dripping, and breathing fire and smoke? I don't. I believe when she saw him, he was "tall, dark, and handsome." He spoke to her in words she could not resist.

When the devil shows up today, and he does, he doesn't look like a monster out of a horror movie. He doesn't show his evil nature. He appears smooth, suave, and debonair. He doesn't frighten; he ENTICES.

After a number of years of missing him on television, I saw him just the other day. I didn't see him literally. I saw Satan appear through one of his ministers. His representative had aged somewhat, but he was still handsome, charming, and had some of the best TV and radio manners I have ever seen. His daddy, who enjoyed the duo status of preacher and politician, is dead and in hell. His father did not believe in hell, but he does now. I thought, "There he is again. He's still damning people. He is still deceiving people by his diction, his charm, his suit and tie, his Bible, his logic and appeal to the intellect."

There is the appeal of appearance, **TO BE SOUNDING LIKE GOD**. I remember a fellow who spoke with such authority, beauty, pronunciation, and gestures that he overwhelmed the crowd:

> **Acts 12:21-22 And upon a set day Herod, arrayed in royal apparel, sat upon his throne, and made an oration unto them. 22 And the people gave a shout, saying, It is the voice of a god, and not of a man.**

Herod was at his best. It was the orator's dream, to have the audience idolize you, deify you in amazement at your prowess. God, however, was not so positively impressed.

> **Acts 12:23 And immediately the angel of the Lord smote him, because he gave not God the glory: and he was eaten of worms, and gave up the ghost.**

Herod had fallen into the trap of Satan. He had desired to be like the most High, to have that appearance in his speaking ability.

There is also the appeal of appearance, **TO BE SEEN AS GOD**. The devil is the greatest counterfeiter of all. He has ministers who LOOK like God's ministers. He has churches which LOOK like God's churches. By the way, many times God's people build churches in homes, storefronts, warehouses, and even tents. The devil knows how to build a church building, though. If you don't believe it, just take a look at your local Mormon church building, your local Kingdom Hall, or your local Catholic church.

The ultimate goal of the appeal of appearance is **TO BE A SUBSTITUTE FOR GOD**. A substitute for God is an antichrist. A substitute for God is an idol. Anything or anyone who can come between you and God is an idol.

Do you recognize the devil? Have you seen him lately? I'm not denying that God is at work in our church. However, contrary to what you might think, the devil is also at work in your church. He is at work in the church down the road. He goes unseen by most people because they don't understand his desire. His desire causes him to transform his appearance...

... and his desire is ... TO BE LIKE THE MOST HIGH. So, he has produced what we will call in this book ...

SATAN'S COUNTERFEITS

CHAPTER 1

AN IMITATION SAVIOR

2 Corinthians 11:1-4 Would to God ye could bear with me a little in my folly: and indeed bear with me. 2 For I am jealous over you with godly jealousy: for I have espoused you to one husband, that I may present you as a chaste virgin to Christ. 11:3   But I fear, lest by any means, as the serpent beguiled Eve through his subtilty, so your minds should be corrupted from the simplicity that is in Christ. 4 For if he that cometh preacheth another Jesus, whom we have not preached, or if ye receive another spirit, which ye have not received, or another gospel, which ye have not accepted, ye might well bear with him.

In this passage, please notice the words, "another JESUS."

As I have already pointed out, the only personality in the Bible who said he wanted to be LIKE God was Lucifer, who made the statement in Isa. 14:14, "...I will be like the most High." That ought to serve as a lesson and a warning to believers who, not knowing what they are saying, proclaim that they want to be LIKE the Lord. The Bible never tells us to have that desire. There is NO command in the word of God for us to be LIKE Jesus. We are merely commanded to be obedient to the Lord and to FOLLOW Him. If you are obedient to the Lord and will follow Him, you may indeed resemble him, but not as an achieved goal, but rather as a by-product of simply being what God would have you to be.

Jesus has been HIGHLY exalted, according to Phil. 2:9, and the verse also states that Jesus has been given a name ABOVE every name. In wanting to be like the most HIGH, the devil wants to be like Jesus Christ. In the above passage in 2 Cor. 11, the apostle Paul referred to the possibility that someone might preach ANOTHER Jesus, whom Paul had NOT preached, to the Christians at Corinth. He was rebuking those carnal Christians for exhibiting a tendency to reject Paul and his apostleship. He accused them of being more willing rather to accept even "another Jesus" whom Paul did not preach. They were more tolerant of error than they were of truth.

The type of compromise practiced by the Corinthians makes it appear that the most heinous sin a person can commit is to publicly expose and censure deceivers and their deceit. This compromise, which is so prevalent today, promotes a tolerance of all kinds of error in doctrine and in practice. This compromise is an ever-spreading illness infecting the body of Christ. May the Lord raise up men of God who will be bold to proclaim the truth, while showing the difference between the holy and the profane, the clean and the unclean, and the true and the false. May the Lord give these men many believers who will band together in support of that message.

The "Jesus" that the devil offers as a counterfeit savior has many characteristics similar to those of the true God and Savior Jesus Christ. If he did not have these characteristics, he would be unable to fool anyone. During the tribulation period there shall be false Christs, and the Bible speaks of "strong delusion" that will come during that time.

> **Matthew 24:24 For there shall arise false Christs, and false prophets, and shall shew great signs and wonders; insomuch that, if it were possible, they shall deceive the very elect.**

Even today there are false Christs. A FALSE Jesus is being preached in churches today, and you should be equipped to recognize him. He is an IMITATION Jesus. He is a COUNTERFEIT Jesus. The "Jesus" the devil presents has many characteristics like the most High. There are, however, some differences, which should be observed by the discerning Christian. The devil is not able to match the Savior perfectly in his imitating powers. His savior, his counterfeit, is flawed, although most people are unaware of the differences. For instance, a little known trait of "another Jesus" who is worshipped today is:

THE IMITATION SAVIOR WAS FORMED IN ETERNITY PAST

The Lord Jesus Christ has no beginning, and He has no ending. Rather, He IS the beginning and the ending, the Alpha and the Omega:

> **Revelation 1:8 I am Alpha and Omega, the beginning and the**

ending, saith the Lord, which is, and which was, and which is to come, the Almighty.

Jesus was in the beginning, according to:

John 1:1-2 In the beginning was the Word, and the Word was with God, and the Word was God. 2 The same was in the beginning with God.

As a matter of fact, Gen. 1:1 says that the earth was created "in the beginning." Bible students understand that Jesus existed before the earth was created. He always WAS, and He always IS. The fact that He was around before the world was made is stated in:

John 17:5 And now, O Father, glorify thou me with thine own self with the glory which I had with thee before the world was.

So, if the earth was created "in the beginning" (Gen. 1:1), and Jesus was with the Father BEFORE the world was (John 17:5), then that means He was not only IN the beginning, but He was BEFORE the beginning, as well! Amen!

CALVIN WAS DECEIVED BY THIS IMITATION SAVIOR. Father of the Reformed theologians, John Calvin taught that Jesus was begotten sometime in eternity past, and in his zeal to contend for this theory, had a man named Servetus executed who denied that idea. (Calvin did want him beheaded rather than burned, which was the manner of his death.) That's right; Calvin believed, as did his hero, Origen, that the following verse meant that Jesus was born sometime in eternity past:

Colossians 1:15 Who is the image of the invisible God, the firstborn of every creature:

Calvin's error was a misinterpretation of the verse. Jesus' identification as "the firstborn of every creature" does not mean that there was a time when He was begotten, or created in eternity past. Rather, it means that He was the firstborn of every creature in that He was the beginning of every creature. He created them. That is, He is the beginning of all things. The Bible is plain in its declaration that all things were made by Jesus Christ, and in the context of the above verse, the very next verse says in:

Colossians 1:16 For by him were all things created, that are in heaven, and that are in earth, visible and invisible, whether they be thrones, or dominions, or principalities, or powers: all things were created by him, and for him:

Notice the word, "For," which begins verse 16. It refers you back to verse 15. Jesus was called "the firstborn of every creature" in verse 15, BECAUSE "by him were all things created"! A similar wording is found in the Book of Revelation:

Revelation 3:14   And unto the angel of the church of the Laodiceans write; These things saith the Amen, the faithful and true witness, the beginning of the creation of God;

Here Jesus is called "the beginning of the creation of God." Does that mean He was created by God before anything else was created? No! It means that, as Col. 1:16 says, "by him were all things created"! Jesus IS the beginning of the creation of God in that He is the beginning of ALL things. ALL things were made by Him, and without Him was not anything made that was made (John 1:3)! He is the Alpha, as well as the Omega. He is the author and finisher of our faith. Jesus is not a CREATURE; He is the CREATOR!

THE CULTS ARE DELUDED, as well. Some of the cults and isms teach that Jesus was just another angel. Some, such as the JFW's (Jehovah's False Witnesses) identify Him with Michael the archangel. Others say He was the brother of Satan. The defective view of Christ's eternal existence is part of what leads the JFW's to believe that He is not truly God, but rather, just a son of God, like other angels.

CHRIST WAS DOGMATIC about the subject. The eternal nature of our Lord is revealed in His statement to the religious leaders of His time in a dispute about Abraham:

John 8:58   Jesus said unto them, Verily, verily, I say unto you, Before Abraham was, I am.

With our finite concepts, it might seem more correct for the Lord to have said, "Before Abraham was, I WAS," but He didn't say that. He said, "Before Abraham was, I AM." You see, in addition to identifying Himself the way that God identified Himself to Moses in Ex. 3:13-14, Jesus was proclaiming His eternal nature. The Lord Jesus Christ not only always WAS, but He always IS! Compare His statement with a similar one made in the Old Testament about God:

Psalms 90:2   Before the mountains were brought forth, or ever thou hadst formed the earth and the world, even from everlasting to everlasting, thou art God.

Again, with the use of the past tense words, "before," "were," and "hadst formed," one would think the verse would end, "thou WERT God." Instead, because God is ETERNAL, it says, "thou ART God." God IS the same yesterday, today, and forever; He IS the God of NOW.

The devil's imitation savior was created. He was not "the beginning," as the true Christ, but he had a beginning. He was formed in eternity past. The TRUE Savior is eternal with neither beginning nor ending. The Lord Jesus Christ is true; the devil's christ is a lie. In addition to this subtle difference, of which the average person is unaware ...

THE IMITATION SAVIOR IS FEMININE

Obvious to Bible-believing fundamentalists, but unobserved by the average church goer, is the fact that the imitation savior, whose portrait has been circulated so well by the devil over the last 20 centuries, has a definitely feminine streak in him. He is not the MAN, Christ Jesus (1 Tim. 2:5), of the Bible. He is "another Jesus" (2 Cor. 11:4). The devil has circulated descriptions of this counterfeit Jesus so well that most people have a mistaken view of the Lord, especially with regard to His manhood. For instance,

THE PAINTINGS PORTRAY JESUS WITH LONG HAIR. I don't believe the painting of Jesus hanging on your wall looks anything like the Savior did while He walked the earth, nor as He looks today. I don't think that He was feminine at all, although that is the way He is usually depicted. I don't think He had rosy cheeks. I don't think He had smooth, soft, Ivory Liquid hands. After all, He was a carpenter and carpenter's assistant for at least two decades! And, by the way, you must remember that there were no power tools back then. Some of you guys build cabinets by going to the store and buying everything "prefabricated." In other words, you put it together like a game or a puzzle (a Tinkertoy set?). I believe Jesus had calluses on His hands.

Concerning fellows who like to wear their hair like women, putting it into a ponytail for church and other occasions for "dress-up," the Bible says,

> **1 Corinthians 11:14 Doth not even nature itself teach you, that, if a man have long hair, it is a shame unto him?**

I think it would be highly ridiculous of the apostle Paul to chew out the Corinthian men for wearing their hair long (and the women for cutting theirs off short), if the Lord Jesus Christ had hair like a woman! God is not like you and me. He doesn't tell us to do as He says, not as He does. Rather, the Bible says,

1 Peter 1:16 Because it is written, Be ye holy; for I am holy.

Jesus led a PERFECT life of sinlessness and holiness. It's a shame for a person to lie, it's a shame for a person to steal, and it's a shame for a man to have long hair. I don't believe the TRUE Lord Jesus Christ was guilty of ANY of those things.

According to 1 Cor. 11, the way a person wears his hair on his physical head shows his submission or rebellion to his authoritative head -- the man to Christ, and the woman to her husband. The Lord Jesus Christ was never in rebellion to the Father, and He never wore His hair long. You say, "Prove it, Preacher." I just did, when I quoted 1 Cor. 11:14. It's a shame, it's a sin, and it's a sign of rebellion when a man wears long hair. Of Jesus the Bible says,

Hebrews 4:15 For we have not an high priest which cannot be touched with the feeling of our infirmities; but was in all points tempted like as we are, yet without sin.

Some say the Lord wore His hair long, because He was a Nazarite. The only problem with that is that "it just ain't so." The Lord Jesus was a Nazarene, being from Nazareth, but He was not a Nazarite. Proof of that is seen in the fact that He approached dead people, and He drank of the juice of the grape. Those actions were forbidden in the Nazarite vow in Numbers 6.

Others who think that Jesus had hair like a woman say that the Old Testament priests were forbidden to get haircuts based on passages like the following:

Leviticus 19:27 Ye shall not round the corners of your heads, neither shalt thou mar the corners of thy beard.

Frankly, I don't believe that verse contradicts 1 Cor. 11:14. There is a difference, I believe, between rounding the corners of your head and getting a haircut. In another place, the Bible says this of the priests:

Ezekiel 44:20 Neither shall they shave their heads, nor suffer their locks to grow long; they shall only poll their heads.

May I suggest that, comparing scripture with scripture, "rounding the corners" of one's head has something to do with "shaving" the head? The priests were FORBIDDEN to allow their locks to grow LONG. They had to poll their heads. The word, "poll," simply means "to cut off or cut short." That is, they were not to shave their heads on the one extreme, and they were not to wear "long hair" (see 1 Cor. 11:14) on the other extreme. They were merely to go to the barber shop every two to four weeks and get a haircut!

For further discussion, see my study booklet, "Hair: the Long and Short of It."

The paintings portray Jesus with woman's hair. Another example of the fact that the counterfeit Jesus of Satan is feminine is seen in the fact that...

THE PANSIES FANCY JESUS AS A SODOMITE, with John as a mate. That's right. One of the lies told by religious queers ("Yes, Mabel; he said, queers,' from the pulpit") is that the Lord Jesus Christ had a "homosexual" (20th century mealy-mouthed terminology for "pervert") relationship with the apostle John. Such blasphemy is motivated by Satan himself. The queers who promote such idiocy are Bible-rejecting fools. Otherwise, they would know that the Lord Jesus Christ was the One who served up "French-fried Fairies" in the destruction of Sodom and Gomorrah.

You say, "Preacher, you certainly are showing a bad attitude toward the gay people." Bad attitude? What are you talking about? I have the RIGHT attitude! After all, GOD was the one who sent the fire down from heaven that sent those Sodom and Gomorrah deviants running around screaming while they burnt to a crisp.

By the way, where did you get that "gay" business, anyway? Sodomites aren't gay; they're queer! The only way I will use the term, gay, is as an acronym, like:

Got AIDS Yet?

God Against You

Gave AIDS Yesterday

Grave Abominable Yoke

Gross And Yucchhh!

Going After Youngsters

You say, "You shouldn't use derogatory names toward them!" Where did you get that idea? Why would you use a GOOD word to describe EVIL people? The Bible is pretty specific in condemning our calling good evil and evil good:

Isaiah 5:20 Woe unto them that call evil good, and good evil; that put darkness for light, and light for darkness; that put bitter for sweet, and sweet for bitter!

These sodomites aren't gay; they're NERVOUS. Why don't you just call them a bunch of "shakes," because they're so nervous? I have had people rebuke me for using a nonscriptural term like "queer" to describe these perverts. Meanwhile, they use an equally nonscriptural term, "homosexual." No, thank you. I'll keep calling them queers, because they ARE queer ("leaving the natural use" -- Rom. 1:27; "against nature" -- Rom. 1:26; "that which is unseemly" -- Rom. 1:27; "not convenient" -- Rom. 1:28). By the way, those of you who are not ignorant about these matters are aware that THEY sometimes use the term "queer" to identify THEMSELVES (Queer Nation, for instance). And before you correct me for using an unscriptural word, you do realize that the word "unscriptural" is not in the Bible, don't you? As a matter of fact, you do realize that the word "Bible" is not in the Bible, don't you? Quit being such a hypocrite about these things!

Don't you know the sodomite Savior proposed by the perverts is just a step toward perversion from the long-haired effeminate Christ portrayed in the paintings? My suggestion is that you get rid of those paintings of "a Savior like the most High." My suggestion is that you discard the foolish notion of Jesus having long hair or being a sodomite.

THE PERVERTS WILL BOW THE KNEE to the MAN Christ Jesus one of these days, according to Phil. 2:10, and they will, too late, confess that Jesus Christ is Lord. They will find that He is "a man of war" (Ex. 15:3) and "Lord of lords" in that day.

> **Revelation 17:14 These shall make war with the Lamb, and the Lamb shall overcome them: for he is Lord of lords, and King of kings: and they that are with him are called, and chosen, and faithful.**
>
> **Revelation 19:11-16 And I saw heaven opened, and behold a white horse; and he that sat upon him was called Faithful and True, and in righteousness he doth judge and make war. 12 His eyes were as a flame of fire, and on his head were many crowns; and he had a name written, that no man knew, but he himself. 13 And he was clothed with a vesture dipped in blood: and his name is called The Word of God. 14 And the armies which were in heaven followed him upon white horses,**

clothed in fine linen, white and clean. 15 And out of his mouth goeth a sharp sword, that with it he should smite the nations: and he shall rule them with a rod of iron: and he treadeth the winepress of the fierceness and wrath of Almighty God. 16 And he hath on his vesture and on his thigh a name written, **KING OF KINGS, AND LORD OF LORDS.**

Related to the difference in manhood between the Lord Jesus Christ and the savior "like the most High," is the fact that

THE IMITATION SAVIOR IS FRAIL

Don't be fooled. The Savior "like the most High" has been publicized so widely that most people wouldn't recognize the TRUE Son of God if He were standing in the room! There is a reason that the Jesus popularized by paintings in Christian bookstores and in Bible story books looks like a weakling. You see, one of the things that the devil hates about the Lord Jesus, I believe, is His great POWER. Therefore, when the devil manufactured his "counterfeit savior," he constructed him to look like a weakling. That's the way he likes to think of Jesus Christ.

The imitation savior is frail **IN HIS PHYSIQUE**. Look at the illustrations of the Lord on your wall or in your family Bible. In most paintings of Jesus, the Lord is portrayed so that he appears to stand about 5'11" tall and weigh about 135 pounds "sopping wet." It is true that Jesus was meek and harmless at His first coming, as the Lamb of God, to be sacrificed for the sins of the world. Meekness, however, is not weakness. I don't think for a minute that the Lord looked like the 98-pound weakling who used to be featured in the Charles Atlas muscle-building ads.

Pilate said to the people, "Behold the man" (Jn. 19:5)! He didn't think of Jesus as a wimp. Nobody else did, either. If anyone gave any indication at all of not realizing what power was at the Lord's command, He straightened them out immediately:

> **Matthew 26:53 Thinkest thou that I cannot now pray to my Father, and he shall presently give me more than twelve legions of angels?**

> **John 10:17-18 Therefore doth my Father love me, because I lay down my life, that I might take it again. 18 No man taketh it from me, but I lay it down of myself. I have power to lay it**

down, and I have power to take it again. This commandment
have I received of my Father.

**Matthew 28:18 And Jesus came and spake unto them, saying,
All power is given unto me in heaven and in earth.**

The imitation savior is frail **IN HIS PREACHING**. The "Jesus" of the
liberals never preaches on hell, judgment, sin, or anything else that might
hurt people's feelings. He never charges His listeners with being "fools"
or "hypocrites" (Mt. 23:14,15,17,19,23,25,27,29). Contrary to the Jesus
of the Bible, the devil's Jesus never gets angry (Mk. 3:5). He doesn't use
derogatory terms to describe people like "serpents", "vipers" (Mt. 23:33),
"dogs" (Mt. 15:26), "swine" (Mt. 7:6). He doesn't accuse people of being
ignorant of the Bible and the power of God (Mt. 22:29).

If the Lord were to deliver a sermon in the flesh in the average church
today, the congregation would rebel against Him and accuse Him of not
having "the sweet spirit of Christ"!

This imitation savior has appeared in the sermons, pictures, and writings
of religion to the extent that the average person has absolutely no idea
that the Lord's preaching was STRONG. I remember years ago when a
backslidden believer sat in church for the first time in years. We were
having a Bible conference, and one preacher after another "shelled the
corn." My guest sat on the front pew next to me, in complete awe. At the
end of each message I asked him what he thought of the messages. He
replied each night with one word: "STRONG!"

The Lord Jesus spoke dogmatically. He spoke authoritatively. Some
people worship a Jesus, a false Jesus, who gives no commandments, only
suggestions. The devils knew firsthand the authority and power of the
proclamations of the Lord:

**Luke 4:36 And they were all amazed, and spake among
themselves, saying, What a word is this! for with authority and
power he commandeth the unclean spirits, and they come out.**

In addition to his authoritative speech, the Lord's speech was unique. As
a man, he was a man among men.

**John 7:44-46 And some of them would have taken him; but no
man laid hands on him. 45 Then came the officers to the chief
priests and Pharisees; and they said unto them, Why have ye**

not brought him? 46 The officers answered, Never man spake like this man.

I believe the average religious teacher in the days the Lord walked the earth was similar in temperament to the average teacher today. The people weren't used to hearing anyone talk like Jesus talked.

The counterfeit savior is frail in his physique, in his preaching and **IN HIS PASSION**. The devil's Jesus never raises His voice, never gets angry, and never gets excited. He is almost passive. Do you remember the story of the cleansing of the temple? Liberals and others who are deceived by the devil, if they were honest about their beliefs, would describe the Lord as prancing into the temple and saying, "Now you children be good boys and run along, please."

A truly modern account of what really happened, especially if the Lord were to do the same thing today, might read more like this:

(BEGIN O'NEAL BIBLICAL SPECULATION) With eyes like a flame of fire, the Lord Jesus Christ glared at the thieves in the temple. Anger swelled within His breast. Walking over to the first bingo table, He placed the heel of his shoe against its edge and with an abrupt, mighty shove turned everything over, causing cards, chips, and players to fall to the floor. From across the room a black-robed priest rose to his feet and shouted with indignation (expletives deleted), "Just who do you think you ARE?"

The Lord answered, "Ye neither know me, nor my Father." Faster than you can say, "Bless me, Father, for I have sinned," the Lord lashed out with His freshly-made whip, catching the hypocrite by his backwards collar, and jerking him over his table, clenched the Baalite's robe in His other hand and drew the frightened man's face up to His own. "If you knew my Father, you would know me," the Lord said. "You have turned my Father's house from a house of prayer into a den of thieves!"

Effortlessly the Lord Jesus flung the worshipper of the Queen of Heaven 20 feet across the room, where he smashed his head into a case of Jack Daniels. Raising His scourge above His head, He addressed the crowd of paralyzed parishioners: "Something BAD is going to happen to you!!!"

They got the message. Their legs spun like buzz saws as they scrambled to get out of the temple.

When the dust cleared, a little fellow of Spanish descent timidly and carefully approached the Lord. "If you don't mind my saying so," he ventured, "I don't think you will win anyone to God that way. I'm a Baptist, too, but you need to show these people the love of God."

"Vinnie," the Lord replied, "you're a wimp. I expect you will stay in the Southern Baptist Convention even when they hold dialogues with these idolatrous rascals. Go hide yourself in a closet for a few years and come see me when you get some sense." (END OF O'NEAL BIBLICAL SPECULATION)

Does that not sound like the Jesus you worship? Could I suggest that perhaps you have a counterfeit savior?

THE IMITATION SAVIOR IS A FAILURE

I didn't see "Jesus Christ, Superstar," but it is my understanding that the musical's conclusion left the Lord Jesus Christ hanging on the cross. It did not cover the glorious victory of the Lord's bodily resurrection. If that's the case, then it is an indication that the "superstar" of the play was not the true Lord Jesus Christ, but rather, a counterfeit.

The devil opposed the atoning work of the Lord Jesus Christ throughout history. Diligent Bible students have pointed out Satan's efforts in Old Testament times, documenting his desire to prevent the coming of the Lord Jesus Christ through the line of Judah. At Christmas each year, millions of people hear the story of how Herod gave a decree to murder all the children two years old and under, in an effort to halt the growth to manhood of the Lord Jesus Christ. It is my personal opinion, by the way, that this is the reason for the emphasis on the BABE at Christmas time rather than on the MAN, Christ Jesus. As a babe, the Lord died for no one. If He had stayed a baby, the devil would have been content. It was as a MAN that our Lord bore the sins of the world upon Himself, died, was buried, and rose again the third day according to the scriptures.

However, it wasn't JESUS who failed, but the DEVIL who failed. Jesus was VICTORIOUS. The devil hasn't stopped his schemes aimed at thwarting the plans of God, but he fails at every turn. This failure has no doubt influenced his depiction of the Lord. Wanting so desperately to cause Jesus Christ to fail, his counterfeit Jesus is something less than the all-powerful Lord Jesus Christ.

The counterfeit savior is, first of all, **UNABLE TO SAVE**. The salvation offered by Satan's savior is not through Jesus, even the false Jesus, directly. Rather, the false Jesus points the troubled sinner to other means for his salvation: baptism, communion, joining the church, keeping the commandments, obeying the Golden Rule, praying the so-called "sinner's prayer," etc. It is as though the blood of Christ were not enough. Speaking of which, two "scholars" of the last generation have boldly declared, "There is nothing in the human blood of Jesus that can save." Both men were led of Satan to proclaim the failure of the blood to redeem man. Both men were preaching the devil's Jesus.

The true Lord and Savior Jesus Christ IS able to save. When He appeared on the scene at John's baptism, an immediate proclamation was made that the Lord Jesus was going to perform by sacrificing Himself what the thousands of sacrifices upon altars through Jewish history had been unable to accomplish:

> **John 1:29 The next day John seeth Jesus coming unto him, and saith, Behold the Lamb of God, which taketh away the sin of the world.**

> **Hebrews 7:25 Wherefore he is able also to save them to the uttermost that come unto God by him, seeing he ever liveth to make intercession for them.**

There is no sinner so wicked that Jesus can't save him! There is no sin so vile that the blood of Jesus Christ can't wash it away! There is no sinner so dead in trespasses and sins that the Son of God cannot raise him from the dead and give him eternal life! There is no sinner so blind that the Light of the world can't enable him to see! There is no sinner so lost that the Way, the Truth, and the Life can't put him on the narrow road! There is no sinner so condemned that our Advocate with the Father cannot secure his freedom! Hallelujah! Contrary to the devil's impotent counterfeit savior, the TRUE Lord Jesus Christ CAN save!

Second, the counterfeit savior is **UNABLE TO SECURE**. Sound Christians know that the salvation of the believer and the security of the believer are actually one and the same thing. Anyone who is saved today is saved eternally, or he is not saved at all. However, some people seem to want to separate the two. Their "Jesus" can forgive them of sins committed in the past, but they have to hold out, hold on, hang on, pray through, live right, and endure unto the end if they're going to make it in the future. These people who worship the devil's Jesus never have assurance of salvation, because they have no true security!

Years ago I spent about 30 minutes talking with a non-Baptist evangelist about the doctrine of the eternal security of the believer. Don't take offense, but I believe 99% of these people are lost. One of the men in my church had been dealing with a coworker about salvation, and he had agreed to go to the man's church for a revival service. He asked if I would go with him, in case he needed some "back-up." After the man was finished preaching, he came to my pew and asked what I thought of his message. Needless to say, he had really made a mess out of the Bible. He was as mixed up as a termite in a yo-yo. He had just tried to teach that the apostolic gifts were being distributed today.

I spent a little time talking with him from the word of God about the gifts, especially tongues, after which he became frustrated and said, "I have a book in my study that will tie you up in knots about this issue."

I replied, "I have a book in my LAP that will tie you up in knots, friend. Why don't we just go by IT?"

He said, "Listen, one of the greatest Bible scholars of all time, J. Finnius Dake, believed tongues are for today."

"I wouldn't expect Dake to be right on the subject of tongues," I answered. "He wasn't even grounded on the doctrine of eternal security. How can you expect a man to be right on the gifts of the Spirit when he doesn't even understand the gift of salvation and eternal life?"

Well, that "got it going." We went back and forth. The man gave one hypothetical situation after another. You know: "What if a person got saved and went home and shot his wife?" I gave him one scripture after another. It was sad to see that this man, who obviously had read a number of religious books, was so ignorant of THE Book, the Bible. He was just as blind as Nicodemus was in John 3. He said, "I read a verse the other day that will settle this argument. Turn to Romans 9:3."

I obliged.

"That's not it," he said. "Turn to Romans 10:3."

We looked at that one.

"That's not it, either. It's somewhere."

He browsed through the book of Romans, frantically looking for a verse that teaches you can lose your salvation. As he began to wear down, I said to him, "You know what your problem is, sir?"

"What?"

"Your problem is Romans 10:3, which you had me turn to just a moment ago. Let's go back and look at it."

Romans 10:3 For they being ignorant of God's righteousness, and going about to establish their own righteousness, have not submitted themselves unto the righteousness of God.

"Your problem is that you're trying to establish your OWN righteousness by your works. You will NEVER be saved until you submit unto the righteousness of GOD, which is by FAITH in Jesus Christ."

A few minutes later, he finally began to give up. He said, "You know, if I believed like YOU believe, I don't guess I would have a thing to worry about!"

"NOW you're getting it!" I said. "Here, read this." I gave him a tract called, "You May Be Religious, But Are You Saved?" and I left the church with my church member.

Listen, my friend: God saves, and He saves with an ETERNAL salvation. When a person obeys from the heart the gospel of Jesus Christ, He receives an everlasting salvation:

Hebrews 5:9 And being made perfect, he became the author of eternal salvation unto all them that obey him;

The security available to the believer in Jesus Christ is compared to being held in His all-powerful hand:

John 10:27-30 My sheep hear my voice, and I know them, and they follow me: 28 And I give unto them eternal life; and they shall never perish, neither shall any man pluck them out of my hand. 29 My Father, which gave them me, is greater than all; and no man is able to pluck them out of my Father's hand. 30 I and my Father are one.

If your savior isn't able to secure your soul for all eternity, you have the WRONG savior! The apostle Paul used the argument of God's perpetual love to explain the security of the believer:

Romans 8:38-39 For I am persuaded, that neither death, nor life, nor angels, nor principalities, nor powers, nor things present, nor things to come, 39 Nor height, nor depth, nor any other creature, shall be able to separate us from the love of God, which is in Christ Jesus our Lord.

Therefore he could say with assurance,

2 Timothy 1:12 For the which cause I also suffer these things: nevertheless I am not ashamed: for I know whom I have believed, and am persuaded that he is able to keep that which I have committed unto him against that day.

Third, the imitation savior is **UNABLE TO STRENGTHEN**. He is unable to help people have the strength to go to church, to tithe, to endure trials and temptations, to take a job for Him, or to quit bad habits. The Bible speaks of the inability of the devil's false prophets, who will be examined in Chapter Six, to do right:

2 Peter 2:14 Having eyes full of adultery, and that cannot cease from sin; beguiling unstable souls: an heart they have exercised with covetous practices; cursed children:

On the other hand, the Lord Jesus Christ, the TRUE Savior, is able to equip the believer to do anything and everything God wants him to do. The apostle Paul knew this, and even in jail he testified, as we find written in:

Philippians 4:13 I can do all things through Christ which strengtheneth me.

When a worshipper of the false Christ gets into a battle, and his back is up against a wall, he will find that the power of Satan is limited. To the contrary, when a believer finds that NO ONE else will stand with him and encourage him, when he has NO ASSISTANCE as far as eye can see, he still has HELP, praise God, from the one genuine Savior! The apostle Paul knew what it meant to be deserted, even by Christian people, and to be left alone in a time of trial. Yet he found that in his isolation, as he wrote in:

2 Timothy 4:17 Notwithstanding the Lord stood with me, and strengthened me; that by me the preaching might be fully known, and that all the Gentiles might hear: and I was delivered out of the mouth of the lion.

GLORY!

Finally, this imitation savior is a failure in that he is **UNABLE TO SUPPLY**. The devil's wells eventually run dry, but the Lord Jesus Christ has an ABUNDANT supply of LIVING water, amen! When He was walking the earth, the Lord entered into a conversation with a woman, the oft-referred-to "woman at the well," who had spent her life serving an IMITATION savior. Oh, yes, she was religious, and she was willing to get into a theological discussion with the Lord. The truth was, however, that she had been married five times, was "shacked up" with a man at the time, and she was seeking for things that could not satisfy. Jesus, who knows all things, knew the woman's nature, He knew the woman's need, and He spoke to her of His ability to supply in:

John 4:13 Jesus answered and said unto her, Whosoever drinketh of this water shall thirst again: 14 But whosoever drinketh of the water that I shall give him shall never thirst; but the water that I shall give him shall be in him a well of water springing up into everlasting life.

When the prophet's widow ran out of money, God supplied. When there was no food to serve to the multitudes who followed Jesus, God supplied. When there was no money to pay the taxes of the Lord and His disciples, God supplied.

The imitation savior runs out of supplies, much like the servants ran out of wine at the marriage in Cana of Galilee in John 2. You may get into a period of your life when it looks as if there is just no way to make ends meet. It may appear that your funds and provisions have been cut off. But if you are a child of God through our Lord and Savior Jesus Christ, the Bible says:

Philippians 4:19 But my God shall supply all your need according to his riches in glory by Christ Jesus.

The Psalmist said:

Psalms 37:25 I have been young, and now am old; yet have I not seen the righteous forsaken, nor his seed begging bread.

God has only promised to provide our NEEDS, not our desires, and our needs are two: food and raiment. When Jesus illustrated the ability of God to supply our needs, He spoke of the clothing of the lilies of the field, and the feeding of the fowls of the air. The New Testament says:

1 Timothy 6:8   And having food and raiment let us be therewith content.

If your savior is unable to supply the basic needs of life specified above, then YOU HAVE THE WRONG SAVIOR. You have a failure for a savior.

In review, the devil's imitation savior 1. was formed in eternity; 2. is feminine; 3. is frail; and 4.is a failure. Don't be fooled! The devil is able to pull off some clever tricks, and he imitates God pretty closely. He has AN IMITATION SAVIOR.

CHAPTER 2

AN IMITATION SALVATION

Galatians 1:6-10 I marvel that ye are so soon removed from him that called you into the grace of Christ unto another gospel: 7 Which is not another; but there be some that trouble you, and would pervert the gospel of Christ. 8 But though we, or an angel from heaven, preach any other gospel unto you than that which we have preached unto you, let him be accursed. 9 As we said before, so say I now again, if any man preach any other gospel unto you than that ye have received, let him be accursed. 10 For do I now persuade men, or God? or do I seek to please men? for if I yet pleased men, I should not be the servant of Christ.

It is my intention in writing this book to demonstrate that for nearly EVERYTHING that the Lord has, the devil, who is the greatest imitator of Christ of all time, has a COUNTERFEIT.

This is due to his desire to "be like the most High." Among those things that the devil has copied is the Lord's salvation. The Lord has a salvation, and it is a wonderful salvation. The Bible calls it "so great salvation" in Heb. 2:3.

Hebrews 2:3 How shall we escape, if we neglect so great salvation; which at the first began to be spoken by the Lord, and was confirmed unto us by them that heard him;

The devil offers a salvation LIKE that of the most High. It is not the same as God's salvation, and it does not have the same excellence or effects as does God's salvation, but it is nevertheless, LIKE God's salvation. In the above scripture, Paul warned about "another gospel." He also made reference to the possibility of "another gospel" when he wrote to the saints at Corinth about Satanic counterfeits:

2 Corinthians 11:4 For if he that cometh preacheth another Jesus, whom we have not preached, or if ye receive another

spirit, which ye have not received, or another gospel, which ye have not accepted, ye might well bear with him.

Someone had come into the church at Galatia and was troubling Paul's converts, perverting the gospel of Christ. The reason that the perverted message could be called "another gospel" and yet also be said to be "not another" is that the word, "gospel," means "good news." This definition can be determined by comparing Rom. 10:15 with Isa. 52:7.

Romans 10:15 And how shall they preach, except they be sent? as it is written, How beautiful are the feet of them that preach the gospel of peace, and bring glad tidings of good things!

Isaiah 52:7 How beautiful upon the mountains are the feet of him that bringeth good tidings, that publisheth peace; that bringeth good tidings of good, that publisheth salvation; that saith unto Zion, Thy God reigneth!

The gospel is GOOD NEWS. Someone at Galatia had taken the GOOD news that salvation is offered as a free gift, having been purchased by the sacrificial death, burial, and resurrection of the Lord Jesus Christ and had PERVERTED that message. These wicked, religious seducers were preaching "another gospel" to the people of Galatia. Their gospel stated that in order for a person to STAY saved, he had to be circumcised and keep the Old Testament law. That is, some deceivers had turned the GOOD news of the gospel into news that was not good at all. So it was not in reality another GOSPEL. There was an effort by Satan's ministers to remove the Galatian converts from the gospel Paul had preached to them, which he defined in 1 Cor. 15. Paul began that chapter, a chapter that was primarily written to defend the truth of the resurrection, by saying:

1 Corinthians 15:1 Moreover, brethren, I declare unto you the gospel which I preached unto you, which also ye have received, and wherein ye stand;

Pay attention. If you want to know the content of the gospel Paul preached, he is about to define it:

1 Corinthians 15:3-4 For I delivered unto you first of all that which I also received, how that Christ died for our sins according to the scriptures; 4 And that he was buried, and that he rose again the third day according to the scriptures:

It is a sad fact that many professing Christians have neglected the epistles of Paul in their Bible reading and study. They have majored in books, and it is not our intent to minimize the inspired, infallible nature of these books (ALL scripture is given by inspiration of God - 2 Tim. 3:16), such as Proverbs, or Matthew, Mark, Luke, and John, and overlooked the books of Romans, 1 & 2 Corinthians, Galatians, Ephesians, Philippians, Colossians, 1 & 2 Thessalonians, 1 & 2 Timothy, Titus, and Philemon, books which focus primarily on truth for Gentile believers in the church age. The fruit of this neglect of the New Testament epistles of Paul is that entire churches are unacquainted with the gospel of the grace of God, as preached by the apostle Paul.

The events recorded in the narrative of Matthew, Mark, Luke, and John were what led up to the wonderful deliverance which is actually expounded and explained in the Pauline epistles. It is true that our deliverance comes through what Jesus did in those first four books of the New Testament, but PRIMARILY through what He did in the very END of each book. Although the virgin birth and sinless life of Jesus Christ were required in God's redemptive plan, the salvation which we enjoy was made available when our Lord Jesus Christ shed His blood on an old rugged cross, taking our sins upon Himself in his own body; when He was buried, and when He rose again. Although the events are recorded in the four gospels, the IMPACT of that atoning work is detailed in the writings of Paul, especially in Romans, Galatians, and Ephesians.

Those who find fault with the doctrine of God's eternal salvation, offered to sinners as a gift through faith without works of any kind, are generally more familiar with Ezekiel than they are Romans, and with Matthew than they are Ephesians. Anyone who has dealt firsthand in house to house soul-winning with these lost religionists knows what it is to regularly encounter a rejection of Romans 4:5 and 5:1 due to a misunderstanding of Ezekiel 18:24, or a rejection of Ephesians 2:8,9 due to a misapplication of Matt. 24:13.

Even though we are 2,000 years down the road, and there has been ample opportunity for every believer to perceive and proclaim the wonderful salvation offered through the Lord Jesus Christ, there are many people today who have accepted a salvation which is "LIKE that of the most High," but is not THAT of the most High. That is, they received the DEVIL'S IMITATION salvation. I want to remind you that the devil wants to be LIKE the most High. He is NOT the most High, but he wants to IMITATE the most High. His salvation is not the salvation which is of God, but it is one that is LIKE that of God.

THE DEVIL'S IMITATION SALVATION RESEMBLES THAT OF THE SAVIOR

The salvation offered by Satan so closely resembles that which is offered by the Lord and Savior Jesus Christ that it has deceived the religious world into thinking that it is indeed the salvation of God. I'm reminded of the deception, allowed by God and administered by Satan, which will be so strong in the coming Tribulation period which follows the Rapture of the church:

> **2 Thessalonians 2:10-12   And with all deceivableness of unrighteousness in them that perish; because they received not the love of the truth, that they might be saved. 11 And for this cause God shall send them strong delusion, that they should believe a lie: 12 That they all might be damned who believed not the truth, but had pleasure in unrighteousness.**

Those who reject the truth will open themselves up for "strong delusion" in the Tribulation period. I believe that people who reject the truth of God today are susceptible for the deception Satan is spreading in our day, through counterfeit "plans of salvation."

THE DEVIL'S IMITATION SALVATION APPEARS TO BE RIGHTEOUS

We often refer to the devil's crowd as "wolves in sheep's clothing." That is due to the fact that the apostle Paul warned the Ephesian elders of the forthcoming invasion of wolves who would attack the flock.

> **Acts 20:29   For I know this, that after my departing shall grievous wolves enter in among you, not sparing the flock.**

As I will point out in another chapter, if you want to know what a Christian should look like, don't go to your typical Baptist church. Too many believers in this day of compromise and conformity (Rom. 12:1,2) have tailored their appearance to match the fashions of this world. If you want to see how a Christian should appear, examine one of the devil's missionary teams, such as a pair of Mormons. They will usually have close haircuts, dark slacks, and a white shirt and tie.

To digress a moment, let us give a brief explanation for any reader who might not recognize that the Mormon church is not a Christian church. I want you to understand that the Mormons preach a perverted gospel. Mormon missionaries are not saved.

A couple of their missionaries entered my house many years ago, saying they were ministers of the gospel of Jesus Christ. They sat down on my couch and related a tall tale about a man named Joseph Smith, some supernatural eyeglasses, some special plates containing new revelations from God, a visit by Jesus Christ to the American Indians, and some other things. When they were done, I addressed them:

"When you fellows knocked on my door, you said that you were ministers of the gospel of Jesus Christ. I listened to your presentation, but I never heard you refer to that gospel. Maybe I missed it. Exactly what do you think the gospel of Jesus Christ IS?"

You never saw two more uncomfortable young men in all your life. After they offered a few guesses which I told them were incorrect, they finally asked, "Well, what do YOU think the gospel is?"

I turned over to 1 Cor. 15:1-4 and read the account. I then turned to Gal. 1:6-9 and emphasized the importance of preaching the gospel Paul preached and the curse that is placed upon those who preach another gospel. Before you could say, "Polygamy," or "Holy Underwear!" those counterfeit ministers were GONE! I wonder why the passage bothered them so much?

> **Galatians 1:6-9 I marvel that ye are so soon removed from him that called you into the grace of Christ unto another gospel: 7 Which is not another; but there be some that trouble you, and would pervert the gospel of Christ. 8 But though we, or an angel from heaven, preach any other gospel unto you than that which we have preached unto you, let him be accursed. 9 As we said before, so say I now again, if any man preach any other gospel unto you than that ye have received, let him be accursed.**

Too many Christians are ignorant of the background and teachings of the Mormon church. All they know is what they have seen on the television commercials purchased by the organization. They aren't acquainted with the Mormon revelation that special undergarments with a Masonic-looking emblem on them will protect them from spiritual and physical harm. I'm not kidding. One of the peculiarities of the Mormons is that they wear holy underwear! I know: you have just discovered that YOU may be a Mormon, too.

The devil's salvation will almost always make use of the Bible. It will refer to living for God and keeping His commandments. It will emphasize performing good works and abstaining from evil. It will usually stress water baptism. It will often make reference to the Holy Spirit. It appears righteous.

THE DEVIL'S IMITATION SALVATION ANNOUNCES ITS REALITY

Preachers of the devil's gospel and the devil's salvation claim that what they have is real. They sometimes claim that if you get what they have, you can FEEL it. This appeals to many numb Christians who attend petrified churches, because they haven't felt anything since they were spanked on the bottom in the hospital delivery room. As a fellow said, "Jesus said that many are called but few are chosen, but in MY church, I am afraid that many are COLD, and a few are FROZEN!"

Concerning those adherents of the devil's salvation, there is some veracity in their claim of reality. The spirit world is not tangible, but it is real, and it can indeed affect the emotions, which in turn affect one's body. If a person is in a non-Christian religious service, he is probably having religious, spiritual experiences indeed. When a person responds at the closing invitation in a service at a non-Christian church, he kneels, he prays, and he often feels something. He may even hear a voice speak to his heart. The problem is, he's in a church LIKE God's church, he has heard a message LIKE God's message, he has felt a conviction LIKE God's conviction, and he has heard a spirit LIKE God's Spirit. Unfortunately, he has been hoodwinked into thinking he has been in touch with God.

I remember attending a tent meeting in my days of training as a minister. An "older preacher" (he must have been at least 29 or 30 at the time) was with me. There was more confusion in the service than you could shake a stick at. I was shocked at it all. Also a little shocking was the fact that when the preacher would say something about God in his sermon, my elder brother would cup his hand to his mouth and shout up to the man, "Wrong God! ... god of this world!"

THE DEVIL'S IMITATION SALVATION APPEALS TO THE RELIGIOUS NATURE OF MAN

You see, man is religious. A fellow says, "I am just not a religious person." He's a liar. Even atheists are religious. They are religious FOOLS (Ps. 14:1), but they are religious.

Psalms 14:1 The fool hath said in his heart, There is no God. They are corrupt, they have done abominable works, there is none that doeth good.

God calls atheists fools. That's because of what they PROFESS. They say there is no God. They don't BELIEVE that; they just BROADCAST that. In their hearts, they know better. They are fools, because they REJECT in their hearts what God has REVEALED to their hearts. But they are still religious.

YOU'RE religious. You may not attend church, but you have religious beliefs. You think some things are right and other things are wrong. You have opinions about death, God, outer space, paranormal phenomena, and the treatment of your fellow man. Don't tell ME you're not religious.

The devil's imitation salvation appeals to the religious nature of man. It provides him with a system of beliefs. It equips him with a guidebook. It supplies him with a spiritual counselor.

The devil's imitation salvation resembles that of the Savior. This is due to his desire to be "like the most High." In spite of the similarities, there are some distinct differences between the counterfeit salvation of Satan and the genuine, great salvation offered by the God of heaven. In this book I want to point out likenesses and differences so that you will be aware of what is happening in the spirit world. For instance, one characteristic of the devil's imitation salvation is that:

THE DEVIL'S IMITATION SALVATION REMOVES THE SHED BLOOD OF CHRIST

You see, one of the great components of God's "so great salvation" (Heb. 2:3) is the precious blood of the Son of God, shed for our sins on Calvary's cross. We Christians sing about it. We sing, "What can wash away my sins? Nothing but the BLOOD of Jesus. What can make me whole again? Nothing but the BLOOD of Jesus." We sing, "My hope is built on nothing less than Jesus' BLOOD and righteousness." We sing, "Would you be free from your burden of sin? There's power in the BLOOD, power in the BLOOD." We sing, "Saved by the blood of the crucified one ... glory! I'm saved! Glory! I'm saved! My sins are all pardoned; my guilt is all GONE!"

Some popular Bible teachers of my generation have said we Christians were deceived about the merits of the literal blood of Christ because of hymns containing such words as those above. Is that so?

Pardon me if I get a little carried away here. You see, we Christians feel very strongly about the blood of our Lord. The reaction of God's people to that heretic's remarks was so staggering that he shortly came out with a sequel article, called something like, "I Believe in the Precious Blood." You had better believe in the precious blood. Whether or not that man changed his mind, clarified his previous writings, or just lied due to pressure from saved people is still the subject of debate. But there is really no room for debate about the REQUIREMENT of blood redemption or the REALITY of blood redemption.

Excuse me if you think I am chasing a rabbit on this point. If there is anything on which I might "go to seed," it is the subject of salvation through the precious blood of the Lord Jesus Christ. The Bible says,

> **Romans 3:25 Whom God hath set forth to be a propitiation through faith in his blood, to declare his righteousness for the remission of sins that are past, through the forbearance of God;**

When I trusted Christ, I put faith in His BLOOD that was shed for me. What did you trust to wash away your sin?

> **Romans 5:9 Much more then, being now justified by his blood, we shall be saved from wrath through him.**
>
> **Ephesians 1:7 In whom we have redemption through his blood, the forgiveness of sins, according to the riches of his grace;**
>
> **Ephesians 2:13 But now in Christ Jesus ye who sometimes were far off are made nigh by the blood of Christ.**
>
> **Colossians 1:14 In whom we have redemption through his blood, even the forgiveness of sins:**

We have been JUSTIFIED by His blood, REDEEMED by His blood, and MADE NIGH by His blood. This is not some delusion common among Christians because of misguided song writers. This is the authoritative teaching of scripture!

Colossians 1:20 And, having made peace through the blood of his cross, by him to reconcile all things unto himself; by him, I say, whether they be things in earth, or things in heaven.

Hebrews 9:12 Neither by the blood of goats and calves, but by his own blood he entered in once into the holy place, having obtained eternal redemption for us.

Bible-believing Christians understand and accept the doctrine of the eternal security of the believer. Part of our understanding comes from an acceptance of the work of the blood of Christ in obtaining "eternal redemption for us."

Hebrews 9:14 How much more shall the blood of Christ, who through the eternal Spirit offered himself without spot to God, purge your conscience from dead works to serve the living God?

Hebrews 9:22 And almost all things are by the law purged with blood; and without shedding of blood is no remission.

Hebrews 10:19 Having therefore, brethren, boldness to enter into the holiest by the blood of Jesus,

I hope that you're beginning to realize that the subject of the blood atonement is a main theme of the Bible. The fact that the Devil's salvation doesn't emphasize Christ's blood in its message is very significant.

Hebrews 10:29 Of how much sorer punishment, suppose ye, shall he be thought worthy, who hath trodden under foot the Son of God, and hath counted the blood of the covenant, wherewith he was sanctified, an unholy thing, and hath done despite unto the Spirit of grace?

Hebrews 12:24 And to Jesus the mediator of the new covenant, and to the blood of sprinkling, that speaketh better things than that of Abel.

Hebrews 13:12 Wherefore Jesus also, that he might sanctify the people with his own blood, suffered without the gate.

Hebrews 13:20 Now the God of peace, that brought again from the dead our Lord Jesus, that great shepherd of the sheep, through the blood of the everlasting covenant,

1 Peter 1:2   Elect according to the foreknowledge of God the Father, through sanctification of the Spirit, unto obedience and sprinkling of the blood of Jesus Christ: Grace unto you, and peace, be multiplied.

God's people are elect through the BLOOD (not THROUGH foreknowledge; they are elect ACCORDING to foreknowledge).

1 Peter 1:18-19   Forasmuch as ye know that ye were not redeemed with corruptible things, as silver and gold, from your vain conversation received by tradition from your fathers; 19 But with the precious blood of Christ, as of a lamb without blemish and without spot:

1 John 1:7   But if we walk in the light, as he is in the light, we have fellowship one with another, and the blood of Jesus Christ his Son cleanseth us from all sin.

That verse says the "blood of Jesus Christ his Son cleanseth us from all sin." "Cleanseth" is a present tense verb. It describes a present progressive act. The blood is NOT just a theological concept! The blood is at work TODAY, cleansing believing sinners in a permanent salvation and cleansing saints in a progressive sanctification.

Revelation 1:5   And from Jesus Christ, who is the faithful witness, and the first begotten of the dead, and the prince of the kings of the earth. Unto him that loved us, and washed us from our sins in his own blood,

Revelation 5:9   And they sung a new song, saying, Thou art worthy to take the book, and to open the seals thereof: for thou wast slain, and hast redeemed us to God by thy blood out of every kindred, and tongue, and people, and nation;

They sing about the blood of Christ and its power in heaven! Do you think THEY'RE deluded? Who do you suppose authored the song of Revelation 5:9???

Another characteristic of this counterfeit salvation which often appears is:

THE DEVIL'S IMITATION SALVATION REPLACES THE BLOOD WITH WATER

People who think they can wash their sins away by being dunked in the baptistry (such as the Church of Christ, the Christian Church, the Catholics, and most of the rest of them) remind me of Pilate, the governor, who was in between the proverbial rock and a hard place. He was afraid to crucify Jesus, and he was afraid to release Him. Under pressure he gave Jesus into the hands of those who would slay him.

> **Matthew 27:24 When Pilate saw that he could prevail nothing, but that rather a tumult was made, he took water, and washed his hands before the multitude, saying, I am innocent of the blood of this just person: see ye to it.**

The washing of his hands in water was symbolic, but he thought in doing so he was rid of the guilt that he felt in delivering Jesus to be crucified. He was no more cleansed from his sins than is your average unsaved Baptist who gets rebaptized every Spring Revival meeting, just because it makes him FEEL better about himself!

There are people who think that they can get into the baptismal fount and go to heaven. Their problem is that they have never been in, as the song says, the "fountain filled with blood, drawn from Immanuel's veins." They can't DO it. YOU can't do it. You may get into the baptismal fount, but in order to go to heaven, you must be washed in the BLOOD, "and sinners plunged beneath THAT flood lose ALL their guilty stains." Hallelujah!

I believe every Christian should be baptized as a testimony of what happened to him when he got saved and as a testimony of what saved him (the substitutionary death, burial, and resurrection of the Lord Jesus Christ), but you had better be SURE that the first washing you experienced was the washing in the BLOOD of the Son of God! Otherwise, you will just be another baptized, hell-bound Baptist.

The Campbellites (That's another name for the Church of Christ, to whom I sometimes refer as Campbellites, after their founder, Alexander Campbell. I also call them Southern Catholics because of their mutual belief in baptismal regeneration.) like to quote 1 Pet. 3:20, which says that in the days of Noah eight souls were saved by water. Well, an exposition of that passage will take more time and space that I care to take here, but I will point out that the ONLY people who benefitted from the water in Noah's day in ANY sense of the word, were FIRST ... IN THE ARK.

Did you get that? Everyone who got into the WATER without getting into the ARK ... PERISHED! Likewise, if a person gets into the baptistry without first getting into Christ, he is going to hell and will burn forever. On the other hand, if a person gets into CHRIST, he will never perish, even if, like Noah and his family, HE NEVER EVEN TOUCHES THE

WATER. Friend, you need to get into the ARK! The ark of safety is the Lord Jesus Christ Himself, not some church pool of water! Then, and ONLY then, are you ENTITLED to get into the baptismal waters.

A number of years ago I had been witnessing to a fellow, but he never would trust Christ. Nor would he visit my church. One Monday I saw him and he said, "Brother Mike, I just wanted you to know that I got baptized yesterday."

In those days I wasn't too tactful (I since have matured into a model of tact, poise, and gentleness in dealing with people), and my response to him was, "What did you go and do a thing like THAT for?"

"Well, I just thought it was the thing to do," he answered. He didn't KNOW why he was baptized. He couldn't say he did it as a testimony of his newfound faith in Jesus Christ, because he hadn't trusted in the crucifixion of Christ; he just trusted in the so-called Church of Christ. He hadn't been BORN AGAIN; he had just been BAPTIZED. He couldn't even say he was baptized because he had been saved, because he thought the baptism itself was what saved him.

Water baptism for salvation is the devil's substitute. The devil has talked many people into getting baptized who were concerned about their soul. Don't get me wrong; I believe in baptism. After all, I AM a BAPTIST. As I have often said, if you ask me what I would be if I were not a Baptist, I would be ASHAMED. But water baptism does not put you in Christ.

THE DEVIL'S IMITATION SALVATION REPLACES THE BLOOD WITH WORKS

Those duped by the devil might sing, "I'm building a bridge." They might sing, "If anyone makes it, Lord, surely I will." They perform works in hope of securing heaven at the end of their lives. All of this is, of course, in vain. The works of a Christian do not purchase his salvation. You can do all of the things a Christian should do -- praying, reading the Bible, soul-winning, etc. -- and die and go to hell. On the other hand, a person can refuse to pray, read his Bible, get baptized, or any OTHER Christian work, and still go to heaven, because the Bible says:

Romans 4:5 But to him that worketh not, but believeth on him that justifieth the ungodly, his faith is counted for righteousness.

THE DEVIL'S IMITATION SALVATION REPLACES THE BLOOD WITH WISHFUL THINKING

A false hope of salvation is in reality only wishful thinking. When a man thinks he is going to be justified before God because he has kept the sacraments, been baptized, been confirmed, joined the lodge, been good to his fellow man or paid his bills, he is merely exercising wishful thinking. Only the BLOOD can make an atonement for the soul.

> **Leviticus 17:11 For the life of the flesh is in the blood: and I have given it to you upon the altar to make an atonement for your souls: for it is the blood that maketh an atonement for the soul.**

When God delivered the children of Israel from Egypt, He instructed every household to apply the blood of a lamb to their homes. Those who applied the blood escaped destruction. The families who thought that they could avoid God's wrath without applying the blood experienced DEATH in EVERY home. God said, "When I see the BLOOD, I will pass over you" in mercy.

Those who think they can avoid God's wrath in eternity without trusting in the shed blood of Christ to wash away their sins are going to find out too late that "without shedding of blood is no remission" (Heb. 9:22).

Another characteristic feature of the counterfeit salvation of Satan is that:

THE DEVIL'S IMITATION SALVATION REWARDS THE SINNER FOR GOOD DEEDS

Little did the children of Israel know that the devil had given them a counterfeit of God's true salvation. Endeavoring to receive righteousness by the works of the law, they failed miserably, entirely ignorant of the righteousness of God, which is received by faith. The heart of the apostle Paul was broken over his kinsmen according to the flesh. He wrote by inspiration of God:

> **Romans 10:1-3 Brethren, my heart's desire and prayer to God for Israel is, that they might be saved. 2 For I bear them record that they have a zeal of God, but not according to knowledge. 3 For they being ignorant of God's righteousness, and going**

about to establish their own righteousness, have not submitted themselves unto the righteousness of God.

The Israelites of Paul's day were some of the most religious people on the face of the earth, but they were lost. They were trying to earn salvation by good deeds. Such is the state of American Christendom. Churches are full of unsaved religionists, people who have never been born again by the Spirit of God, although they maintain a form of godliness.

Paul prayed for those lost Jews, that they might be saved. Today I pray for lost Baptists, that they might be saved. I pray for lost Methodists, that they might be saved. I pray for lost charismatics, Campbellites, and Catholics, that they might be saved. I pray for lost Pentecostals and Presbyterians, that they might be saved.

Are YOU saved? Should we be praying for you? If I asked you what you are counting on to get you to heaven, would you tell me about something that YOU did, or something that JESUS did? A man listened to me preach the other day, and he indicated he had doubts about his salvation because one preacher would say one thing, and another preacher would say something else. I asked him what he believed that he had to do to be saved. His answer was, "Just stay in the word of God." Do you see what I mean? That man was trusting what HE was doing; that's why he had no assurance of salvation. By the way, the man I talked to is a Baptist. What kind of Baptist? The LOST kind!

THE DEVIL'S IMITATION SALVATION PRESENTS A PLAN INSTEAD OF THE MAN, CHRIST JESUS

Our message is not: Do this, do that, and do the other thing, and you will be qualified to go to heaven. Our message is Jesus Christ. Our message is the man Christ Jesus.

Philip didn't preach a plan to the people of Samaria. He preached a MAN:

Acts 8:5 Then Philip went down to the city of Samaria, and preached Christ unto them.

Philip didn't preach a plan to the Ethiopian eunuch; he preached a MAN:

Acts 8:35 Then Philip opened his mouth, and began at the same scripture, and preached unto him Jesus.

Paul didn't preach a plan after he became a Christian; he preached a MAN:

Acts 17:18 Then certain philosophers of the Epicureans, and of the Stoicks, encountered him. And some said, What will this babbler say? other some, He seemeth to be a setter forth of strange gods: because he preached unto them Jesus, and the resurrection.

There is one God, and there is one mediator between God and men, the man, the Man, the MAN -- CHRIST JESUS. I don't BELIEVE in a PLAN of salvation; I believe in the MAN of salvation. If there IS such a thing as a plan of salvation, it was accomplished by the MAN of salvation, the Lord Jesus Christ, when He died for our sins according to the scriptures, was buried, and rose again the third day according to the scriptures!

I was witnessing to a lady today who said, "Preacher, you know that if you were to go to different churches, they would give you different plans of salvation." She was right. But we don't preach a PLAN; we preach a PERSON!

All over America the blind are leading the blind, teaching them that they must accomplish a number of things in order to be saved. I asked a lost preacher (yes, even preachers need to be saved) to tell me what I need to do to be saved. He answered, "Well, if you will tell me what you have done so far, I will tell you what you are still lacking!" You may think that I'm kidding you, but that's not a joke. That's really what he said!

THE DEVIL'S IMITATION SALVATION PROMOTES PRIDE INSTEAD OF THE MASTER

Beware of those who try to bestow assurance of salvation through some study course that puffs up the mind. On numerous occasions I have asked people if they were saved, and I have been told, "No, but I am studying to be." What they meant was that they were taking a study course with the Jehovah's Witnesses, the Roman Catholic Church, the Church of Christ, the Worldwide Church of God, or some other group, in hope of eventually graduating with a certificate of completion and confidence of going to heaven. You don't have to take a 10-week study course to learn how to become a Christian; you can learn how to become a Christian in less than 10 minutes!

The devil's imitation salvation leads a person to think that he's going to heaven because he has achieved something by his own intellectual or physical achievements. In contrast to that, the Bible says,

> **Ephesians 2:8-9 For by grace are ye saved through faith; and that not of yourselves: it is the gift of God: 9 Not of works, lest any man should boast.**

THE DEVIL'S IMITATION SALVATION PROVIDES PAYMENT INSTEAD OF MERCY

That is, Satan tricks people into thinking that they can somehow earn their salvation. The Bible does not teach that a saved person gets what he deserves. It is the mercy of God that thankfully FREES him from getting what he DOES deserve -- hell! God's salvation is provided through the merit of the Lord Jesus Christ! The devil's salvation, which is only a COUNTERFEIT salvation or deliverance, is provided through the goodness of the sinner! It establishes the righteousness of the sinner by his own good deeds. GOD'S TRUE salvation is provided through the goodness of the Savior! It bestows the righteousness of God to the believing sinner!

THE DEVIL'S IMITATION SALVATION RESULTS IN SORROW

When you make a choice of any consequence, you should consider, What will be the result of my choice? Where will it lead? What are the benefits? What are the penalties?

I know some of you have a hard time accepting as a fact my proclamation that most preachers on television are lost. You have seen them cast out devils, raise the sick, and do many wonderful works. Listen, however to the words of the Lord Jesus concerning such charlatans:

> **Matthew 7:22-23 Many will say to me in that day, Lord, Lord, have we not prophesied in thy name? and in thy name have cast out devils? and in thy name done many wonderful works? 23 And then will I profess unto them, I never knew you: depart from me, ye that work iniquity.**

That is one of the most significant passages in the entire Bible! Just this week a dear friend asked me how charismatics could be wrong and still be able to do such wonderful works as healing people and casting out devils. Although I maintain that nearly ALL so-called "wonderful works" of the charismatics today are nothing more than fakery and entertainment, the Lord Jesus Christ said that some preachers who claimed to be doing many wonderful works, including casting out devils, were in reality working iniquity! Look again at the above passage! He did not just say that SOME people would be doing this; He said MANY would do so! Did you get that? God said that MANY people will be in hell who claimed to do supernatural miracles in the name of the Lord!

By the way, if God were in this business of blowing on people so that they fall backwards (see any Benny Hinn crusade), there would be no need for personal workers to catch the people as they fall. Surely God would not allow them to be hurt as a result of getting "a touch from God"! You say, "Preacher, do you mean that you don't believe in Benny Hinn's ministry?" Answer: Not any more than I believe in "championship wrasslin'."

You say, "I just can't believe they're phonies."

Aw, grow up! Have you never been fooled in a romantic relationship? Have you never been fooled by a military recruiter? Have you never been fooled by a salesman? Then why in God's name do you think you can't be fooled in the SPIRITUAL realm? Why don't you give the devil credit for being craftier than any salesman? Why do you think that the Bible commands repeatedly, "Be not DECEIVED"?

Jesus said, "I never knew you." He did not say, "I once knew you, but you backslid, and you lost your salvation." He said He NEVER knew them. He was talking about people who NEVER had God's salvation. They claimed to have it, but they FAKED it! He spoke of people who were not His sheep. They were not His ministers. They were SATAN'S ministers, disguised as ministers of righteousness. The whole time they were prophesying in JESUS' name, casting out devils in JESUS' name, and doing many wonderful works in JESUS' name, they were actually working iniquity.

May God use this study to open your eyes to the fact that the devil is the greatest trickster who has ever existed. You need to be very, very careful. You need to be sober. You need to be vigilant (1 Pet. 5:8).

THE DEVIL'S IMITATION SALVATION RESULTS IN DOUBTS IN THE HEAD

One of the joys of God's salvation is the blessed assurance of which the songwriter spoke and of which the Bible testifies:

> **1 John 5:13 These things have I written unto you that believe on the name of the Son of God; that ye may know that ye have eternal life, and that ye may believe on the name of the Son of God.**

That is not to say that a saved person never doubts his salvation. If that were so, 1 John 5:13 and the scriptures to which it refers would have never been written, for they would have been unnecessary. I am not saying that if you doubt your salvation, you are lost. I believe the devil can deceive believers into doubting God's salvation. But as a general rule, the Lord's salvation is one that is accompanied by much assurance (1 Thess. 1:5), and the devil's counterfeit salvation brings little assurance. This is primarily due to the fact that Satan's imitation salvation rests upon the wisdom and works of man rather than upon the power of God.

When religious counterfeits go to bed at night, they sometimes are plagued with doubt, unsure of their destiny if they were to die in their sleep. They have fears as they face surgery and the prospect of being put to sleep. They are troubled with their own insecurities at the funeral of a loved one.

THE DEVIL'S IMITATION SALVATION RESULTS IN DEADNESS IN THE HEART

Unsaved people may have feelings, leadership, stirrings, and motivation from unclean spirits which indwell them, but they are still dead inside. The Bible says they are DEAD in trespasses and sins (Eph. 2:1). Even when they are having physical enjoyment, they are still dead:

> **1 Timothy 5:6 But she that liveth in pleasure is dead while she liveth.**

Even when they are filled with unclean spirits, unsaved people are EMPTY of what they really need for inner satisfaction and fulfillment. The woman at the well in John chapter four was seeking for satisfaction and could not find it, for she was seeking it from the things that this world has to offer. She had gone through Husbands 1, 2, 3, 4, and 5, only to forsake the marriage vows altogether in disgust and "shack up" with a man. Even in that life of pleasure, she was still dead. But when she met JESUS, Hallelujah, she found the well that never shall run dry! She ran through the city, telling all the men of the city who knew her life of debauchery, "I met a MAN! I met a MAN! I met a MAN who told me all things that ever I did! Is not this the Christ?" Yes, she met the man, the one man who was the one mediator between God and man, the GOD-man, Christ Jesus.

THE DEVIL'S IMITATION SALVATION RESULTS IN DAMNATION IN HELL

Jesus will say to those religious impostors, "DEPART FROM ME!" Don't be fooled by the devil's salvation. Don't go to the lake of fire, because you allowed Satan to slip you a counterfeit. Recognize that all of your righteousnesses are as filthy rags. Acknowledge that you are spiritually bankrupt, without God and without hope. Then trust the Lord Jesus Christ, who died for our sins according to the scriptures, was buried, and rose again the third day according to the scriptures.

If you will believe on the Lord Jesus Christ, you can sing, "It's real! It's real! Oh, I know IT'S REAL! Praise God, the doubts are settled! And I know, I know IT'S REAL!" Not only will it be a REAL salvation, but it will be the RIGHT salvation, for it will be GOD'S salvation.

For many years, my policy was that missionaries who come to speak as guests at our church would first fill out a questionnaire. This was a form that each of our supported missionaries filled out each year. In that questionnaire is the following question:

13. The proper instruction of a missionary to a heathen who asks,

"What must I do to be saved?" is

A. invite Jesus into your heart B. repent of your sin

C. believe on the Lord Jesus Christ D. be baptized E. confess

Christ before men F. all of the above G. other

Those who know their Bibles should recognize both the question and the answer. They come from the 16th chapter of the book of Acts, which contains the story of the Philippian jailor. That lost man got concerned about his soul.

Acts 16:29-31 Then he called for a light, and sprang in, and came trembling, and fell down before Paul and Silas, 30 And brought them out, and said, Sirs, what must I do to be saved? 31 And they said, Believe on the Lord Jesus Christ, and thou shalt be saved, and thy house.

Do you know that MOST of the missionaries who filled out the questionnaire gave the wrong answer? It's unbelievable! The only missionaries who ever contact me are fundamental missionaries, too! I don't get contacted by the liberals, for some reason. I want to ask these missionaries, "Why are you not satisfied with the answer given by Paul and Silas?"

If missionaries, preachers, and evangelists cannot give the correct answer to the question, "What must I do to be saved" on a written questionnaire, you can be CERTAIN that they are not giving the right answer in personal work and in their sermons. That's sad! It's no WONDER people in the pew are confused! The men in the pulpit are PERVERTING the message of the gospel of salvation and are instead offering the DEVIL'S salvation! It's CLOSE to that salvation of the most High; it's LIKE that of the most High; however, it will not save a sinner from his sins, damnation, and hell. Beware of the devil's IMITATION SALVATION. It is one of SATAN'S COUNTERFEITS!

CHAPTER 3

AN IMITATION SPIRIT

2 Corinthians 11:4 For if he that cometh preacheth another Jesus, whom we have not preached, or if ye receive another spirit, which ye have not received, or another gospel, which ye have not accepted, ye might well bear with him.

All true Christians understand that the Holy Spirit is God, even as the Lord Jesus Christ is God, and as the Father is God. To neglect the Holy Spirit is a grave mistake. A believer needs to learn and appreciate Him, if he is going to be all that he should be as a Christian. It is true that the Spirit of God was not sent to exalt Himself. It is a fact that a Spirit-filled person will testify of Christ rather than the Holy Spirit. However, the Bible has much to say about God the Holy Ghost, and we are to live by EVERY WORD of God (Lk. 4:4). So, we need to know what the Bible teaches about the Spirit of God.

Notice in the above verse that the apostle Paul referred to the fact that the carnal Corinthian believers might receive "another spirit," which they had not received. In other words, they had already received the Holy Spirit, also known as the Holy Ghost as well as many other names in God's word. There was the possibility, though, that they might receive ANOTHER spirit. As a matter of fact, the gist of Paul's statement was that they would be more likely to receive an unclean spirit than they would receive him as an apostle. His statement is filled with sarcasm, as is much of this chapter.

There is a danger in ignoring the spirit world. If a believer is unlearned in this vital subject, he may think that all of his problems have to do with the world and the flesh. Another hindrance exists, however, to our Christian walk. That hindrance is the devil. Notice that our primary difficulties, and our foremost battles are not in the realm of the flesh, but that of the spirit:

Ephesians 6:12 For we wrestle not against flesh and blood, but against principalities, against powers, against the rulers

of the darkness of this world, against spiritual wickedness in high places.

There is an additional danger of recognizing the realm of the spirit, but still being very ignorant of it. Since, as we have already observed, the devil is in the business of counterfeiting the things of God, it should come as no great surprise that he has "a spirit like that of the most High." Once again, the devil has come up with a counterfeit so close to the real thing that he has fooled millions of people. As close as the devil's imitation spirit is, however, there are some distinguishing characteristics that any trained believer can spot when dealing with the spirit world. I want to point out some things in this chapter that identify that UNHOLY imitation of the HOLY GHOST.

IT IS A DEVILISH SPIRIT

There are two kinds of spirits in this world: the Spirit of God, and the spirits of devils. The Bible says,

> **Luke 4:33 And in the synagogue there was a man, which had a spirit of an unclean devil, and cried out with a loud voice,**

These devilish spirits are **NUMEROUS**. I believe the average Christian looks upon devils as simply a subject of fundamentalist theology. In other words, devils are something you contemplate for a Bible study, but they are not experienced in daily activities. Practically speaking, this is no different from the modernist who views devils simply as an evil influence; i.e., the devil of strong drink, the devil of gambling, etc. This is a serious error. I am convinced that there are MULTITUDES of devilish spirits in the world. I believe that every unsaved person has at least one of them, for the Bible says,

> **Ephesians 2:1-2 And you hath he quickened, who were dead in trespasses and sins; 2 Wherein in time past ye walked according to the course of this world, according to the prince of the power of the air, the spirit that now worketh in the children of disobedience:**

From the above verses it is obvious that every unsaved person has a devilish spirit. Actually, I believe some lost people have more unclean spirits than do others. Concerning the devil-possessed man of the Gadarenes, the Bible records these words from an exchange between the Lord Jesus Christ and the spirits within the afflicted man:

Mark 5:8-9 For he said unto him, Come out of the man, thou unclean spirit. 9 And he asked him, What is thy name? And he answered, saying, My name is Legion: for we are many.

Even as God's Holy Spirit has various names and is a PERSON (not merely God's "active force" as the Jehovah's Witnesses perverted scriptures read in Gen. 1:2), these devilish spirits are **NAMED** -- they have personalities. The above spirit was called "Legion." He had that name because he represented MANY. That man had MANY unclean spirits.

These spirits are all devilish, but some are more wicked than others. Notice the truth as it was proclaimed by the Lord Jesus Christ:

Matthew 12:45 Then goeth he, and taketh with himself seven other spirits more wicked than himself, and they enter in and dwell there: and the last state of that man is worse than the first. Even so shall it be also unto this wicked generation.

Therefore, not only do some people have more spirits than do others, but also some people have spirits who are more wicked than spirits possessed by others. This refutes the error that some people vigorously propagate by statements like "all sins are equal," and "one sin is as bad as another." No, that's wrong. Some people are more wicked than others, and some sins are greater than others. Note again the authoritative words of the Lord:

John 19:11 Jesus answered, Thou couldest have no power at all against me, except it were given thee from above: therefore he that delivered me unto thee hath the greater sin.

This truth needs to be emphasized. People who are unsaved may appear religious, moral, and good, but they are indwelt by WICKED, DEVILISH SPIRITS. They are not good people who are just lacking one more good thing, that is, to trust Christ (how many times have you heard that type of expression used to describe a lost Pharisee?). They are BAD people, possessed with BAD, devilish spirits!

IT IS A DISGUSTING SPIRIT

Revelation 18:2 And he cried mightily with a strong voice, saying, Babylon the great is fallen, is fallen, and is become the

habitation of devils, and the hold of every foul spirit, and a cage of every unclean and hateful bird.

Devilish spirits are compared to foul, unclean, and hateful birds. They resemble the Holy Spirit, unless you get to see them "up close." Look up in the sky and you may see a majestic-looking, large bird overhead. As it glides through the air gracefully, the bird's appearance may stir you to say, "That's beautiful." However, I've seen those birds after they have landed. I have lived in the country, and I have often come upon those birds as they were having lunch at the Roadkill Cafe. I'm talking about BUZZARDS. Watch one of those creatures as he sits atop a decaying dog on the side of the road, and you'll realize that he's not as beautiful as you thought. Watch him pull the entrails out of a two-day-old corpse, and you'll think twice before paying him a compliment on his appearance. Gross, man.

THIS IMITATION SPIRIT IS UNGODLY

The Lord is not leading unsaved people. As I will shortly point out from scripture, unsaved people are led by the god of this world, not by the Holy Spirit. Therefore, the motivation inside them is not of God, but of Satan. This is difficult for some Christians to accept, when they see lost religious pretenders who seem to maintain some degree of outward morality. However, Jesus said of them:

Matthew 23:28 Even so ye also outwardly appear righteous unto men, but within ye are full of hypocrisy and iniquity.

Inside many of the preachers who may be viewed on any given Sunday on television or on some so-called "Christian" television and satellite networks on a daily basis, dwells a spirit that is just as wicked, hateful, and rebellious against God as you could imagine.

These birds, these unclean spirits, are "up to no good." If they are ever present for the preaching or teaching of the word of God, it is for the purpose of STEALING God's words out of the hearts of those who hear them! If you have any doubt about the comparison of unclean spirits to birds, perhaps you will be convinced by these words of the Lord Jesus Christ:

**Mark 4:3-4 Hearken; Behold, there went out a sower to sow:
4 And it came to pass, as he sowed, some fell by the way side, and the fowls of the air came and devoured it up.**

Perhaps you remember that parable of the sower and the seed. In the interpretation of the above lines from His parable, the Lord explained it this way:

> **Mark 4:14-15 The sower soweth the word. 15 And these are they by the way side, where the word is sown; but when they have heard, Satan cometh immediately, and taketh away the word that was sown in their hearts.**

THIS IMITATION SPIRIT IS UNCLEAN

While Pentecostal evangelist Jimmy Swaggart was holding his tent meetings and crusades across the country, making fun of Baptists, he was chasing whores in cheap motels. While he and Jim Bakker, the charismatic founder of Praise the Lord network (affectionately tagged by the discerning believer as the "Pull The Leg" network) who was also caught in immorality, emphasized the Holy Spirit, perhaps their listeners would have done well to put the emphasis on the HOLY rather than on the SPIRIT. I'm afraid that Swaggart and his cronies got the WRONG spirit. Jesus said:

> **Matthew 23:27 Woe unto you, scribes and Pharisees, hypocrites! for ye are like unto whited sepulchres, which indeed appear beautiful outward, but are within full of dead men's bones, and of all uncleanness.**

Did you read that? WITHIN, the scribes and Pharisees were FULL of ALL UNCLEANNESS! Given enough rope, a religious hypocrite will eventually hang himself, and given enough time, he will eventually expose himself.

In my first church, I was driving our guest evangelist through our town. We passed by a charismatic church which boasted that it was the fastest growing church in the entire county. My preacher friend asked, "Has he committed adultery yet?" I said, "Well, he did, but it was some time ago. He has since remarried, and was called to this church." "It will happen again," the preacher said. "Just give him time." He was right. You don't go for too many years courting the spirits of devils and stay clean, brother!

THIS IMITATION SPIRIT IS UNHEALTHY

Like a buzzard, it has been feeding on dead, rotten things for a long time. It is destructive, robbing a man of his physical health, his peace of mind, his joy, his character, his reputation, and even his family. If you are a believer, you had better be a careful discerner of spirits. As one fellow said, "All ghosts ain't HOLY!" These birds are deadly, and although they may not manifest themselves in that way, they will pick and pick and pick at their prey until there is nothing left.

1 Peter 5:8 Be sober, be vigilant; because your adversary the devil, as a roaring lion, walketh about, seeking whom he may devour:

IT IS A DYNAMIC SPIRIT

Revelation 16:14 For they are the spirits of devils, working miracles, which go forth unto the kings of the earth and of the whole world, to gather them to the battle of that great day of God Almighty.

I maintain that 99% of ALL so-called miracles performed by the ministries of the charismatic conmen are a hoax. However, the previous verse is plain in its declaration that spirits of devils can work MIRACLES. Anyone who doesn't believe this doesn't know the devil's devices as much as he thinks he does. The devil's BIGGEST work is DECEPTION, and one means of accomplishing this is the performance of miracles. Most people are so ignorant of the scriptures that they automatically assume that anything that looks like a miracle must have come from God.

Unfortunately for the gullible and unlearned, DEVILS can work miracles. I'll cover the Bible teaching on this FACT in Chapter Eight in this book called, "Imitation Signs and Wonders." Therefore, I'll not go into great detail here about the kinds of miracles that are performed by Satan.

I just want to mention a few areas in which the power of this "spirit like that of the most High" manifests itself. For instance, a study of the word of God on this subject reveals that the devil and his devils are **ABLE TO GIVE SUPERNATURAL STRENGTH**. This is evident from the record of Mark 5.

Mark 5:2-4 And when he was come out of the ship, immediately there met him out of the tombs a man with an unclean spirit, 3 Who had his dwelling among the tombs; and no man could bind him, no, not with chains: 4 Because that he had been often bound with fetters and chains, and the chains had been

plucked asunder by him, and the fetters broken in pieces: neither could any man tame him.

Second, they are **ABLE TO GIVE SUPERNATURAL SIGNS**. These will be used by devils in the tribulation period to deceive people and entice them into worshiping the antichrist. These will be more than just sleight-of-hand tricks. These will be MIRACLES. The antichrist will use this power in the coming Tribulation Period to damn people to hell who rejected the gospel during the church age:

> **2 Thessalonians 2:8-10 And then shall that Wicked be revealed, whom the Lord shall consume with the spirit of his mouth, and shall destroy with the brightness of his coming: 9 Even him, whose coming is after the working of Satan with all power and signs and lying wonders, 10 And with all deceivableness of unrighteousness in them that perish; because they received not the love of the truth, that they might be saved.**

Third, they are **ABLE TO GIVE SUPERNATURAL SECRETS**. See Deut. 13:1-3 which covers such phenomena as fortune tellers, palm readers, and their ilk, who sometimes seem to have supernatural revelation about a person's private life or his future. It explains that ESP (Extra-Sensory Perception), remote viewing, and mind reading may have more to do with spiritism than it does with science.

IT IS A DIRECTING SPIRIT

The Bible teaches that every believer is led by the spirit of God. This does not mean that each believer FOLLOWS that leadership, but the fact is, God's Holy Spirit is inside the child of God, leading him into the way of righteousness.

> **Romans 8:14 For as many as are led by the Spirit of God, they are the sons of God.**

Likewise, the devil works in HIS children, the unsaved (John 8:44). Why do unsaved people do the things they do? It is that they are directed by "a spirit like that of the most High."

> **Ephesians 2:2 Wherein in time past ye walked according to the course of this world, according to the prince of the power of the air, the spirit that now worketh in the children of disobedience:**

As the Holy Ghost leads the believer to worship God, the devil leads the unbeliever to worship SATAN. His work is so crafty that his captive usually thinks he is worshiping the true God, while in reality he is serving the god of this world, Satan. That is, this spirit leads people to **REPLACE GOD'S SAVIOR** with the devil!

> **1 Corinthians 12:2 Ye know that ye were Gentiles, carried away unto these dumb idols, even as ye were led.**

Worship occurs in the realm of the spirit. Many people are successful in contacting the spirit world in their worship, and they assume that they are engaged in something right and good, because they know they are experiencing something that is REAL. However, it is not enough just to worship in the spirit. God is looking for people to worship Him in spirit, but that's not all:

> **John 4:23-24 But the hour cometh, and now is, when the true worshippers shall worship the Father in spirit and in truth: for the Father seeketh such to worship him. 24 God is a Spirit: and they that worship him must worship him in spirit and in truth.**

God is seeking people to worship Him in spirit and in TRUTH.

As God's Spirit gives the fruit of love, joy, peace, longsuffering, gentleness, goodness, faith, meekness, and temperance (Gal. 5:22,23), the devil gives imitations of those attributes to His children. They are by nature inferior to that of the Holy Spirit, but they are close enough to satisfy, at least temporarily, the unregenerate disciple. Artificial fruit, if constructed carefully enough, almost looks just like the real thing. However, if you try to EAT that fruit, you will be sorely disappointed. Likewise, the devil has counterfeit fruit of the spirit, but they are not able to truly satisfy. It has been said that "all of Satan's apples have worms."

Additionally, the devilish spirit will lead the unwary **TOWARD REBELLION AGAINST GOD'S SCRIPTURES** and **TOWARD RESISTANCE AGAINST GOD'S SPIRIT**. When the word of God is being preached publicly, and when a gospel witness is being given privately, there is a SPIRITUAL WARFARE going on.

> **Ephesians 6:12 For we wrestle not against flesh and blood, but against principalities, against powers, against the rulers of the darkness of this world, against spiritual wickedness in high places.**

IT IS A DOCTRINAL SPIRIT

The Lord Jesus Christ promised His disciples that when He returned to the Father in heaven, He would send the Holy Ghost to teach them. This was absolutely necessary, as a casual reading of the gospel accounts will reveal. It is amazing to see how the disciples were unable to understand the mission of the Lord Jesus Christ when He walked the earth. Yet, later, they were able to understand all things, because of the advent of God's Holy Spirit:

> **John 16:13 Howbeit when he, the Spirit of truth, is come, he will guide you into all truth: for he shall not speak of himself; but whatsoever he shall hear, that shall he speak: and he will shew you things to come.**

> **1 John 2:20 But ye have an unction from the Holy One, and ye know all things.**

Similarly, the devil's spirit is a teaching spirit. The Bible warned of this:

> **1 Timothy 4:1 Now the Spirit speaketh expressly, that in the latter times some shall depart from the faith, giving heed to seducing spirits, and doctrines of devils;**

In the following verses in 1 Timothy, the Bible makes it clear that the Roman Catholic Church has been under the influence of Satan for nearly two millennia, because the description of the "doctrines of devils" matches some of the teachings of Rome!

Have you not noticed that some of the major cults and isms entice unstable souls into their fold through "Bible studies?" JFW's (Jehovah's False Witnesses) are some of the most "studying" people you'll ever run into! Did you know that the Mormons study? Many members of the heretical group known as the Church of Christ (sometimes called "Campbellites" by Bible believers, because they were founded by Alexander Campbell) study the Bible much more than do true born-again Christians. The Seventh Day Adventists were born out of Bible studies led by unclean spirits.

Any dedicated soul-winner knows that the members of the various counterfeit Christian cults have all learned a number of the same heresies. The Campbellites, the JFW's, the Morons (oops, I mean, Mormons), all know how to use James 2 to prove that a person can lose his salvation if he doesn't work. They all know how to use Matt. 24:13 to prove that same heresy. A soul-winner really does not need to spend a lot of time studying how to handle the objections of any particular cult, because they all are led by the same spirit! Therefore, although they all have their idiosyncrasies (baptism for the dead, holy underwear, no blood transfusions, British-Israelism, etc.), on IMPORTANT issues, such as salvation by the grace of God, there is not a hair's bit of difference between them.

The spirit of the devil primarily teaches false doctrines through two means. The first is **COUNTERFEIT "BIBLES."** Please see Chapter Five on "Imitation Scriptures." The new "bibles" deviate from the King James Bible on more things than just the "thee's" and "thou's." If you check them, as I have, you will find that they change verses that deal with some of the most important doctrines of the Christian faith! This practice of CORRUPTING the word of God was widespread even as early as the days of the apostle Paul, and today these bogus "bibles" are on every hand.

> **2 Corinthians 2:17 For we are not as many, which corrupt the word of God: but as of sincerity, but as of God, in the sight of God speak we in Christ.**

These unclean spirits are not content to promote these "bastard bibles," as David Otis Fuller used to call them, among the ranks of unsaved people. They are actively engaged in enticing saved people, as well, especially preachers and teachers of the word of God, into laying aside the King James Version in order to pick up one of the devil's "bibles." Proud and rebellious children of God sometimes open themselves up to the direction of these unclean spirits, and they adopt heresies straight from hell. One of the first places in which this occurs in any Christian group is in the educational institutions organized for the training of Christian ministers. Little do the church members know how the faith of their young men and women is being torn apart in "Bible school." Many parents have sadly watched the faith and orthodoxy of their children be destroyed as they sat under the feet of professors who have given way to unclean spirits in their discourses!

The second means by which this spirit teaches heresy is through **COUNTERFEIT BRETHREN.** These include counterfeit apostles, counterfeit ministers (see Chapter Six on "Imitation Shepherds"), and counterfeit saints (see Chapter Four on "Imitation Saints"). Concerning the inability of these people to provide soul-delivering teaching to their pupils, the Lord Jesus Christ said:

Luke 6:39 And he spake a parable unto them, Can the blind lead the blind? shall they not both fall into the ditch?

All of the studying in the world will not help those who are under the influence of "the imitation spirit." They go to college, they take correspondence courses, they hold home Bible studies, but they are still, as the Bible says in:

2 Timothy 3:7 Ever learning, and never able to come to the knowledge of the truth.

IT IS A DISTRESSING SPIRIT

It **PRODUCES A DISTURBANCE IN THE SOUL.** With all of the things the devil has to offer, he is unable to give the true fruit of the Spirit that fill the heart of the believer. His peace is temporary, his joy goes sour, and his love is actually greed. I knew a dear man who spent a good portion of his life trying to teach positive thinking to people. Yet he confided to me that he was unable to sleep at night without drinking himself to sleep with alcohol.

The devil-possessed man of the Gadarenes was daily in the mountains and in the tombs, crying and cutting himself with stones. He had no real peace.

Mark 5:2-5 And when he was come out of the ship, immediately there met him out of the tombs a man with an unclean spirit, 3 Who had his dwelling among the tombs; and no man could bind him, no, not with chains: 4 Because that he had been often bound with fetters and chains, and the chains had been plucked asunder by him, and the fetters broken in pieces: neither could any man tame him. 5 And always, night and day, he was in the mountains, and in the tombs, crying, and cutting himself with stones.

But what a change JESUS made in his life!

Mark 5:15 And they come to Jesus, and see him that was possessed with the devil, and had the legion, sitting, and clothed, and in his right mind: and they were afraid.

You know, sometimes we attribute a wild, wandering spirit simply to "youth." In other words, we EXPECT young people to be restless. We do not think that it is unusual when they can't sit still for two hours, when they can't hold down a job for more than six months, and when they decide to travel across the country for no reason. Maybe we should wake up to the fact that restlessness is a sign of oppression from "the imitation spirit." When he was full of devils, the man of the Gadarenes was wild, roaming night and day. When he got rid of the devils, he was found SITTING at the feet of Jesus and in his right mind. Amen!

Likewise, the Bible says,

> **Luke 11:24 When the unclean spirit is gone out of a man, he walketh through dry places, seeking rest; and finding none, he saith, I will return unto my house whence I came out.**

Unclean spirits go from one "host" to another, seeking rest. This may give some insight that few people will want to accept about "Attention Deficit Disorder"!

A man came to the Lord Jesus with a troubled son. Maybe you have seen some young people like him. Sometimes for just no reason at all he would go completely nuts.

> **Matthew 17:15 Lord, have mercy on my son: for he is lunatick, and sore vexed: for ofttimes he falleth into the fire, and oft into the water.**

Only an idiot would allow himself to keep falling into fire, unless he's full of devils...

> **Matthew 17:18 And Jesus rebuked the devil; and he departed out of him: and the child was cured from that very hour.**

> **Isaiah 48:22   There is no peace, saith the LORD, unto the wicked.**

This spirit **PRODUCES A DISTRUST IN THE SCRIPTURES**. That has been the work of Satan toward man since the garden of Eden. The first thing that the serpent said to the woman was, "Yea, hath God said...?" (Gen. 3:1). This fact inevitably leads a Bible believer to conclude that most college professors in seminaries are filled with the devil, because MOST Bible college professors don't believe every word of their Bibles. What's more, parents of the students are, although they are generally unaware of what is happening, subjecting their young people to being deceived by the same spirits, as they allow those Deadly Deceivers (D.D.'s) to breathe their unholy falsehoods upon their prey.

The distrust produced in the heart of the individual drives away all hope of God's peace. True peace comes from a mind that is resting on the word of God, and from a heart that loves the word of God.

> **Psalms 119:165 Great peace have they which love thy law: and nothing shall offend them.**

This week I received a tract from an anonymous contributor (I love the courage of these devil-possessed infidels) titled, "The Bible is God's Word?" It has 24 alleged "problems" in scripture and concludes with: "These examples expose only a few of the many reasons I can't accept the Bible as the word of a perfect being." The main reason the fellow can't accept the Bible is that he is as lost as a goose. Second, he's full of the devil. Any fellow who can't "accept the Bible as the word of a perfect being" has been listening to the devil's spirit. You say, "You sure are being judgmental, preacher." You're right, and you should be MORE judgmental. You're COMMANDED to be judgmental in:

> **John 7:24 Judge not according to the appearance, but judge righteous judgment.**

This spirit **PRODUCES DOUBT ABOUT SALVATION**. God has written things for His people so that they can KNOW that they HAVE eternal life:

> **1 John 5:13 These things have I written unto you that believe on the name of the Son of God; that ye may know that ye have eternal life, and that ye may believe on the name of the Son of God.**

All that a person has to do in order to get assurance is to simply believe the RECORD of God's word! In the context of the above verse, immediately before it, we read:

> **1 John 5:10-12 He that believeth on the Son of God hath the witness in himself: he that believeth not God hath made him a liar; because he believeth not the record that God gave of his Son. 11 And this is the record, that God hath given to us eternal life, and this life is in his Son. 12 He that hath the Son hath life; and he that hath not the Son of God hath not life.**

I am very wary of the ministry of preachers who specialize in creating DOUBT about salvation. I am certain that not all professing Christians are saved, but I am not certain that those who make NEW professions of faith have done so as a result of GOSPEL PREACHING (1 Cor. 15:1-4;

Rom. 1:16). Some of these preachers have the same people make three or four professions of faith under their ministry. That is not the work of the Holy Spirit; that's the work of devils. Here's the work of God's Spirit in salvation:

> **1 Thessalonians 1:5 For our gospel came not unto you in word only, but also in power, and in the Holy Ghost, and in much assurance; as ye know what manner of men we were among you for your sake.**

Rather than taking the disturbed church member "one more time" down the "Roman's Road," and before he puts the person once again under the waters of the baptistry, perhaps the preacher could better spend his time examining his spirit and his message. It is likely that he has come under the influence of a "distressing spirit." Unfortunately, the average preacher is very susceptible to such deception from Satan, for the simple reason that he thinks that he is invulnerable.

Bad mistake. The Bible issues a warning directly at those who minister the word of God, and have the souls of men, women, boys, and girls under their care. After admonitions about feeding the flock of God, taking the oversight thereof, and giving a good example, the Bible says "TO THE PREACHER":

> **1 Peter 5:8   Be sober, be vigilant; because your adversary the devil, as a roaring lion, walketh about, seeking whom he may devour:**

I deal with pastors, even fundamental Baptist pastors, on the Internet on a daily basis, who unknowingly have come under the dominion of this "spirit like that of the most High." They know that I am aware of it, even when I don't directly accuse them of it, and it bothers them greatly.

IT IS A DECEIVING SPIRIT

> **1 John 4:1 Beloved, believe not every spirit, but try the spirits whether they are of God: because many false prophets are gone out into the world.**

The spirit of the devil lies to mankind. He leads His children, those who have never believed on the Lord Jesus Christ, to do likewise:

> **John 8:44 Ye are of your father the devil, and the lusts of your father ye will do. He was a murderer from the beginning, and**

abode not in the truth, because there is no truth in him. When he speaketh a lie, he speaketh of his own: for he is a liar, and the father of it.

The devil's spirit fills men with lies. Even Christians are susceptible to this devilish influence. We find an example of that in:

Acts 5:3 But Peter said, Ananias, why hath Satan filled thine heart to lie to the Holy Ghost, and to keep back part of the price of the land?

Before you think that Peter should not have accused another believer of being full of the devil (Satan had filled Ananias' HEART), remember that if ANYONE ought to be acquainted with Satanic pressure, it would be Peter. After all, once Peter spoke out of turn to the Lord Jesus Christ, and he got this back in reply:

Matthew 16:23 But he turned, and said unto Peter, Get thee behind me, Satan: thou art an offence unto me: for thou savourest not the things that be of God, but those that be of men.

When someone lies, the ROOT of the trouble is a devilish, deceitful SPIRIT. Again, this is not just a problem which affects lost people. Saved people lie, as well. When they do, it is because they are full of the devil! The devil, according to John 8:44, is THE FATHER of the lie. Christians who lie are following the wrong spirit!

My life is built around ministering to God's people. I am a pastor. That is my calling. It has been very disturbing to me that in doing the work of an evangelist, that is, in winning people to the Lord Jesus Christ, I find that Christian people are often as deceptive, if not more so, as lost people! How can that be? There is only one answer: The work of this "deceiving spirit" is not limited to the realm of unsaved people.

When the devil first began to deal with men, he approached Eve (women, beware - 1 Tim. 2:12-14) and began to lie to her. One of the things he lied to her about was **JUDGMENT**:

Genesis 3:4 And the serpent said unto the woman, Ye shall not surely die:

Who leads the Seventh Day Adventists to teach soul sleep? Answer: A deceiving spirit. Who instructs the Catholics to believe in purgatory? Answer: A deceiving spirit. Who guides the Jehovah's False Witnesses into their heresy of denying eternal hell fire and torment? Answer: A deceiving spirit.

A deceiving spirit lies about God's judgment. He told Jimmy Swaggart that he could fool around with whores and not get caught. He convinced Jim Bakker that a little fornication wouldn't hurt. And if you have listened to Satan and been deceived about God's judgment, let me take just a moment to remind you of what God has said:

> **Numbers 32:23 But if ye will not do so, behold, ye have sinned against the LORD: and be sure your sin will find you out.**

> **Galatians 6:7   Be not deceived; God is not mocked: for whatsoever a man soweth, that shall he also reap.**

Another thing the devil's spirit lies about is **JESUS**. Without repeating everything we wrote in the previous chapter, suffice it to say that the effeminate Jesus portrayed in 99% of the paintings found in family Bibles and wall paintings is not the Jesus of the Bible. God was not manifest in the flesh as a Frisco fairy; Jesus Christ walked the earth as a MAN. Although He was certainly tender and gentle at times, He also was man enough to go into the temple, make a scourge out of cords, and run everyone out of the building, turning their bingo tables over, with chips flying everywhere (ORV - O'Neal Revised Version).

Lest a believer think that only unsaved people are in danger of being deceived by the devil's imitation spirit, let me issue a solemn warning. There are a lot of spirits in this world besides the Holy Spirit. You and I are engaged in spiritual warfare, and the battleground is your heart and mind. The devil's spirits are REAL. Don't be fooled. Try every spirit out by the word of God. Any spirit that leads you contrary to God's holy word is not of God, but is of the devil.

> **1 Corinthians 10:20 But I say, that the things which the Gentiles sacrifice, they sacrifice to devils, and not to God: and I would not that ye should have fellowship with devils.**

Are you in fellowship with devils? You say, "That's impossible, Brother O'Neal. I'm a fundamental Baptist." I don't care if you're a fundamental, independent, missionary, separated, King James Only, premillennial, pretribulational out-on-the-limb Baptist! You can STILL be in fellowship with devils if you aren't vigilant. That's why 1 Cor. 10:20 was written! That's why 1 Pet. 5:8 was written! Those verses weren't written to unsaved people; they were warnings to SAVED people.

To everyone I warn: BEWARE OF THE IMITATION SPIRIT.

CHAPTER 4

IMITATION SAINTS

The chapter of the Bible that deals with more of the devil's counterfeits than does any other chapter is 2 Cor. 11. In that chapter the apostle Paul "chewed out" the saints at Corinth for their willingness to accept the devil's substitutes for the things of God, and for their UNWILLINGNESS to accept HIS apostleship and its authority. In the second half of the chapter, he gave his "résumé." His credentials were those of persecution and suffering. Consider the following verse, if you will, from among the verses which list Paul's afflictions:

> **2 Corinthians 11:26 In journeyings often, in perils of waters, in perils of robbers, in perils by mine own countrymen, in perils by the heathen, in perils in the city, in perils in the wilderness, in perils in the sea, in perils among false brethren;**

Among the perils in his list of qualifications for the ministry was his persecution and opposition from "false brethren." One application of the term might be toward Christians who were not true in their devotion or service. I believe, however, that he used the word, "false," in reference to the fact that they were not truly "brethren" at all, but were, rather, unsaved religious people who opposed his ministry because they were being controlled and led by Satan. That is, these were LOST people who CLAIMED to be SAVED. They were

IMITATION SAINTS

Paul's antagonists weren't TRUE saints; they were the DEVIL'S saints. They were saints LIKE those of the most High. They were IMITATION SAINTS. The greatest opposition Paul had to his ministry was not from civil authorities. It was not from the worshippers of Diana, although they did give him trouble. It was from people who CLAIMED TO KNOW

GOD. It was from JEWS. Additionally, according to the above passage, he experienced animosity and resistance from "false brethren," people who claimed to be Christians but who really were the children of the devil!

In another scripture, Paul wrote of problems he had with regard to the status of his Gentile "preacher boy," Titus, who was a Greek. There was opposition to the young man's ministry because he was an uncircumcised Gentile. The opposition, as usual, came from "false brethren":

> **Galatians 2:4 And that because of false brethren unawares brought in, who came in privily to spy out our liberty which we have in Christ Jesus, that they might bring us into bondage:**

Probably most of Paul's opposition within the churches was not from carnal or weak Christians, but from "false brethren." If the truth were known, there is a good possibility that the majority of contention and confusion in local churches today is the result of church members who lied their way into the local church. That is, they SAID they were saved, when in reality they had never been born again. They may have transferred their membership from another church, where they were legitimate members on the roll, but they had never had their names on HEAVEN'S roll. It could be that they walked the aisle during the invitation at a church service and filled out a "decision card," but their decision was not to trust the Lord Jesus Christ and His finished work on the cross of Calvary. They took the PREACHER'S hand, but they did not get placed in the hand of the Good Shepherd of John 10:27-30:

> **John 10:27-30 My sheep hear my voice, and I know them, and they follow me: 28 And I give unto them eternal life; and they shall never perish, neither shall any man pluck them out of my hand. 29 My Father, which gave them me, is greater than all; and no man is able to pluck them out of my Father's hand. 30 I and my Father are one.**

I understand that there is a sense in which ALL people are compared to sheep. The term is used that way in Isaiah:

> **Isaiah 53:6 All we like sheep have gone astray; we have turned every one to his own way; and the LORD hath laid on him the iniquity of us all.**

There is another sense, however, in which God compares HIS people to SHEEP, and the DEVIL'S crowd to GOATS. Notice the words of the Lord Jesus, paying special attention to the words, "HIS sheep" and "THE goats."

Matthew 25:32 And before him shall be gathered all nations: and he shall separate them one from another, as a shepherd divideth his sheep from the goats:

The rest of the passage describes the putting of the sheep on the right hand, and the goats on the left. Those on the right, the sheep, went into the kingdom. Those on the left, the goats, went into everlasting fire. This comparison is very significant. Sheep and goats are extremely different, and not only in their diet. Sheep follow better than goats. Do you know that you should not turn your back on an old goat? The reason is that the goat will butt you while your back is turned. A pastor friend of mine from years ago, now with the Lord, Dr. Leroy Wright, was preaching a revival meeting in another town while his deacons (not at his present church, but a former one) burnt down his house back home. Can you believe that? He returned to find his house a smoldering ruin. He returned to find his dogs chained to a tree with their throats cut. Those deacons may have just been rebellious Christians, but I am more inclined to think that they were goats, children of the devil, masquerading as children of God.

These imitation saints are present in every church, in spite of the efforts made by some pastors and their congregations to insure that every applicant for membership is a genuine child of God. These are some of the people who bring shame to the name of Christ and His local church due to their wicked behavior. Sometimes these folks receive church discipline, including having their names removed from the active membership list, when in reality what they need is not discipline as a Christian, but A NEW BIRTH.

These people are NOT church builders; they are church busters. When Paul was an unsaved man, he worked to DESTROY the church. After he came to know the Lord, he worked to DEVELOP churches. Pardon me for assuming, but I just take it for granted that those who hinder the work of God by resisting God's man and God's movement are the devil's crowd, wolves in sheep's clothing.

These imitation saints are a real danger in any church. The Bible likens the infiltration of God's crowd by the devil's agents to the planting of tares among wheat.

Matthew 13:25-30 But while men slept, his enemy came and sowed tares among the wheat, and went his way. 26 But when the blade was sprung up, and brought forth fruit, then

appeared the tares also. 27 So the servants of the householder
came and said unto him, Sir, didst not thou sow good seed in
thy field? from whence then hath it tares? 28 He said unto
them, An enemy hath done this. The servants said unto him,
Wilt thou then that we go and gather them up? 29 But he said,
Nay; lest while ye gather up the tares, ye root up also the wheat
with them. 30 Let both grow together until the harvest: and in
the time of harvest I will say to the reapers, Gather ye together
first the tares, and bind them in bundles to burn them: but
gather the wheat into my barn.

Bible dictionaries tell us that the word "tares" refers to a kind of grass
or weed that flourishes in wheat fields. They are said to be poisonous to
both man and beasts.

The book of Titus warns of people who are UNBELIEVERS, yet
PROFESS to know God:

Titus 1:15-16 Unto the pure all things are pure: but unto them
that are defiled and unbelieving is nothing pure; but even
their mind and conscience is defiled. 16 They profess that they
know God; but in works they deny him, being abominable,
and disobedient, and unto every good work reprobate.

Did you observe that Tit. 1:15 calls them "unbelieving" and Tit. 1:16
says, "They profess that they know God"? These are folks who have the
PROFESSION of salvation, but not the POSSESSION of salvation! They
are "saints LIKE those of the most High." They are the DEVIL'S saints.
They are IMITATION SAINTS. Concerning these "false brethren,"

THEY APPEAR TO BE CHILDREN OF GOD

One of the easiest things for the devil to do is to make his people look
like God's people. In case you are unaware of the difference between the
two spiritual families in this world, let me briefly explain. Until a person
trusts Christ's sacrifice on the cross to take him to heaven, he is spiritually
in the devil's family.

Ephesians 2:3 Among whom also we all had our conversation
in times past in the lusts of our flesh, fulfilling the desires of
the flesh and of the mind; and were by nature the children of
wrath, even as others.

Notice that the verse says that a lost man is by NATURE a child of wrath. Jesus said to lost people in:

John 8:44 Ye are of your father the devil, and the lusts of your father ye will do. He was a murderer from the beginning, and abode not in the truth, because there is no truth in him. When he speaketh a lie, he speaketh of his own: for he is a liar, and the father of it.

When a person trusts Christ, he is saved, born again, and is God's child.

John 1:12 But as many as received him, to them gave he power to become the sons of God, even to them that believe on his name:

Although there may be, yea, SHOULD be, outward manifestations of the inward change that occurs when a person is born again of God's Spirit, the real work of God is on the INSIDE of the person. His soul is saved, and his spirit is born again. Nothing about the flesh changes, other than it becomes a house for the Holy Spirit. People who get saved do not grow a halo. They do not change colors. They look like ordinary people. Therefore, it is a simple matter for the devil to imitate God's saints, because he does not have to change that which only God can truly change -- the inside. People cannot see a saved soul, and they cannot observe a born again spirit. All they can perceive are the fruits or consequences of those changes, and those things can be imitated.

I gave up a long time ago on trying to figure out who is saved and who is not. Nothing surprises me anymore. A fellow who made a public surrender to the ministry in my church had a "falling out" with me and decided to go to another independent Baptist church in our area. One day at the flea market a fellow got my attention: "Hey, Preacher!" After a bit of small talk, he let me know my "preacher boy" was not in church at all. I finally discovered that he was talking vulgar and drinking alcoholic beverages.

Is he saved? I have no idea. When he came to our church he claimed to be a Christian, but his testimony is rather shaky. He once admitted that he may have gotten saved after he started attending our church. I told him if that was the case, he needed to be baptized. He never brought up the subject again.

Another fellow walked the aisle in our church one day. He said God called him to preach. Okay. Unfortunately, his wife was not able to enjoy herself under my ministry, so he left. They went to another independent

Baptist church. Then I received word that he had gotten saved in a revival meeting. "Is that right?" was my response. "In my opinion, the wrong spouse got saved in that meeting." A few weeks later, a teenager from that church told my daughter that the man was going to be preaching that Sunday. The pastor was going to allow him to do it on the occasion of his call to preach. How could that be? Had he not just gotten saved? How was he celebrating an anniversary as a God-called preacher? Was he claiming to be called to preach under my ministry, but got saved later?

Was the man saved? Your guess is as good as mine. When he came to our church he had some Baptist background, but very little. He was as confused as a termite in a yo-yo. He had been involved in Armstrong's Worldwide Church of God teachings and some other off-the-wall stuff. He finally said he was saved but had never been baptized. By the way, his wife, who, I quipped, should have been the one to get saved in that revival meeting, later on DID make another profession of faith.

About a year ago, I heard that the wife of one of my independent Baptist pastor friends here in town had gotten saved. Do I think she really got saved? How should I know? All I can say is, if she WASN'T saved, she sure fooled her husband and all the rest of the church for a number of years!

I believe the reason for a lot of this confusion is that there is a real lack of gospel preaching. I mean that. Fundamental Baptists ought to know and believe the truth. There's not another group that I know of on the earth who is more scriptural in belief and practice than independent, Bible-believing, fundamental Baptist churches. When asked what I would be if I were not an independent Baptist, my answer has always been that I would be ASHAMED!

However, through the devil's work and through tradition, the presentation of the gospel message has suffered greatly. Men who know that salvation is by grace through faith in the finished work of the Lord Jesus Christ on the cross of Calvary obscure that message when they try to answer the sinner's question, "What must I do to be saved?" One of the greatest means by which people obscure the gospel and confuse the sinner is the use of the so-called "sinner's prayer" (see my booklet by that title).

Anyway, Satan has been very successful in camouflaging his disciples, making them look like Christians. For example, the devil's saints appear to be children of God **IN COUNTENANCE**. Everyone knows that an obvious result of being one of God's children is peace and joy inside. Therefore, God's people should appear to be HAPPY people. Our Lord said in:

Luke 10:20 Notwithstanding in this rejoice not, that the spirits are subject unto you; but rather rejoice, because your names are written in heaven.

Since this is the case, Christians should be happy, and they should APPEAR to be happy. If a person is happy in his heart, it should show on his face.

Proverbs 15:13 A merry heart maketh a cheerful countenance: but by sorrow of the heart the spirit is broken.

Happiness is an extremely easy outward characteristic to imitate. It may very well be that the devil's secret emissaries in a local church are some of the "smilingest" people in the assembly! (Yes, Joel ...!) The devil knows that a Christian should be happy, so he directs His people to smile when they are on display! This is not true of ALL of Satan's children, just those who are actively engaged in an effort to be IMITATION SAINTS.

The devil's saints also appear to be children of God **IN CLOTHING**. The whole outward appearance is what is in view in the following verse, but I want to use it in reference to the effort of Satan to dress His saints like God's people.

Matthew 7:15 Beware of false prophets, which come to you in sheep's clothing, but inwardly they are ravening wolves.

Not all of the devil's people have moustaches and goatees, and probably very few of them indeed wear red clothes, horns, and have a pointed tail and hoofs. Rather, they will dress more like a Christian, not necessarily to the extreme of looking exactly like a fanatical, right-wing, Bible-believing fundamentalist, but perhaps more like a faithful member and worker in a church that professes orthodoxy but is part of an apostate movement. In other words, they might look like faithful Southern Baptists or Presbyterians. They will attend church in their "Sunday finest". Their shoes are shined, and their clothes are clean and pressed. They will carry Bibles into church. At a restaurant after church is over, they may even "ask the blessing" (Southern expression for giving thanks) or "say grace" (Northern terminology for the same) over the noon meal.

Look at your typical Mormon missionaries. For years and years they have been bicycling the highways and byways of our towns, recruiting people into their Satanic cult. Do they carry pitchforks? No! They carry

Bibles, books, magazines, and leaflets. Generally speaking, they will wear white or light-colored shirts, ties, and conservative dress slacks. They are not long-haired, chain-wearing, ear ringed slobs with an open shirt and ragged jeans.

The devil's saints appear, as well, to be children of God **IN CLEANLINESS**. The more devout Mormons are known to be people of peculiarity with regard to health and habits, abstaining from coffee, hot tea, liquor, and tobacco. This is also true of the Seventh Day Adventists, who teach many healthy habits. The world thinks that "cleanliness is next to godliness," so the devil's saints generally endeavor to be clean and neat.

Not only do the devil's counterfeit saints APPEAR to be children of God, but also

THEY ACT LIKE CHILDREN OF GOD

"If it talks like a duck and walks like a duck, it must BE a duck." This proverb is based upon our deductive powers with regard to external evidence. Unfortunately, as I said earlier, the "proof of the pudding" with regard to salvation is really INSIDE a person, but nobody can see the inside. We have to form our opinions of what is on the INSIDE of people by what we see on the OUTSIDE. That's why it is important for a Christian to be right on the outside as well as the inside, for what we call "testimony's sake."

> **Matthew 5:16 Let your light so shine before men, that they may see your good works, and glorify your Father which is in heaven.**
>
> **1 Thessalonians 5:22 Abstain from all appearance of evil.**
>
> **2 Corinthians 6:3 Giving no offence in any thing, that the ministry be not blamed:**

The fact that a person's heart is judged by what he does is a theme of the book of James:

> **James 2:18 Yea, a man may say, Thou hast faith, and I have works: shew me thy faith without thy works, and I will shew thee my faith by my works.**

When we observe the imitating work of the devil's saints, we see that they copy the saints of God in that:

THEY SPEAK OF THEIR FAITH

The devil's imitation saints are very vocal while they are active in his service. The Mormon young men who dedicate themselves to two years of missionary activity spend every day trying to tell people about Joseph Smith and the supposed visit of the Lord Jesus to the American Indians. The JFW's (Jehovah's False Witnesses) go out by two's, exactly as the Lord sent His disciples, preaching their false gospel of the kingdom and of justification before God by works. Charismatics buy bumper stickers, car tags, and t-shirts to broadcast their message of holding out, holding on, and enduring unto the end for salvation.

The devil has worked so hard at sending out his disciples by two's, which is, of course, the SCRIPTURAL way for the TRUE gospel to be carried to the public, that this world connects house to house soul-winning with the Mormon and Jehovah's False Witnesses cults. This is a real shame. In my town I have heard on numerous occasions the comment, "You are the first Baptist preacher who has ever knocked on my door," or "I have NEVER known BAPTISTS to go out house to house!"

Another way the devil's saints act like children of God is that:

THEY SING AND SHOUT

The formal, ritualistic form of religion doesn't fool people as much as it once did. People have become convinced that a dead service must represent a dead faith. Therefore, the devil has shifted the activities of his saints to a more emotional exercise of faith.

Even Catholics, who used to impress people with their Latin, chanting, and formal services, have abandoned the old ways in order to act like God's people. This has really been an amazing transformation. When I was studying for the ministry, I could not imagine the possibility of the Catholic Church cross-breeding with the modern charismatic movement. It has happened, however, before my very eyes. That, of course, is a condemnation of the charismatic "glossolalia" error. How could such a movement be of God when it embraces the Great Whore of Revelation

17, that religious system in existence now but will, with modifications, thrive during the Tribulation period, who teaches such heresies as papal infallibility, purgatory, transubstantiation, baptismal regeneration, and the sinlessness of Mary, to mention just a few?

At any rate, the devil has put emotional expression into his disciples, so that they SEEM to have life, the abundant life, gladness, and joy.

> **John 10:10 The thief cometh not, but for to steal, and to kill, and to destroy: I am come that they might have life, and that they might have it more abundantly.**

> **Psalms 32:11 Be glad in the LORD, and rejoice, ye righteous: and shout for joy, all ye that are upright in heart.**

Charismatic churches have really been flourishing since the 1970's, and one of the things that is attracting people is their emotional, high-strung atmosphere.

Of course, they can't do it EXACTLY like God's folks do it. For instance, the unsaved religionists have a hard time singing and shouting about solid hymns of the faith. Most often, they are crying, laughing, and shouting over some new, contemporary piece of music whose arrangement sounds more like country-western music or rock music than it does church music. Nor do they get stirred up and rejoice when a man of God stands up in the pulpit and exposes the errors of the cults and isms.

Another means by which they imitate children of God is that:

THEY "SHARE."

There was a time in the early church when the disciples sold their lands and parted the money to every man as he had need. In an attempt to duplicate this spirit, the god of this world has led people to use the word "share" in place of a number of good words. For instance, instead of "preaching the word," a minister may stand to "share" what God has laid upon his heart. Rather than testifying in a testimony service, the people "share." Rather than teach a truth, a Sunday School class teacher "shares" her thoughts.

This constant "sharing" by the devil's saints is closer to Communism and Socialism than it is Christianity, but it fools a good number of people today, so the devil continues to use this effective tool in imitating the children of God.

Third, the devil has so counterfeited the true saints of the most High so that it can be said of his people,

THEY ASSEMBLE LIKE CHILDREN OF GOD

At a riot in Ephesus, the townclerk tried to subdue the people who were angry at God's soul-winners. He reasoned with them, stating that they were putting themselves in legal jeopardy for their outrageous manner. He said in:

> **Acts 19:37 For ye have brought hither these men, which are neither robbers of churches, nor yet blasphemers of your goddess.**

This verse has caused all kinds of pain to the "Baptist Briders" who reject the infallibility of the King James Bible, because it calls the assemblies of the heathen "churches." Baptist Briders, those Baptists who believe Christ was a Baptist and founded the Baptist Church (see my book, "Blunders and Boo-Boos of Baptist Briders" for the details), have been known to say that only Baptist churches are churches. I have heard them say, "That's the difference between a CHURCH and a CONGREGATION," claiming that non-Baptist churches are only congregations and not churches. Well, this verse "tears them out of the saddle," because it plainly teaches that the heathen God-haters in Acts 19 had CHURCHES.

Yes, the heathen do have churches, and you can find them in the town where you live. The only thing is, you will have to look closely, because the devil's IMITATION SAINTS assemble like children of God.

THEY GATHER IN CHURCHES

The devil knows how to build them, too. Whether it be a Church of Christ (sometimes with a sign saying something like, "Bay Minette Church of Christ -- Founded 33 A.D.," which is very interesting, since there WAS no Bay Minette, Alabama in 33 A.D.), a JFW Kingdom Hall, or a Mormon church building, they are often some of the finest looking edifices in any locality. Some of the larger charismatic congregations have built monstrous, modern pieces of architectural genius, some of which put to shame even city auditoriums and civic centers by their ornate, massive structures.

The devil's imitation saints assemble in their buildings, even as the true saints of God assemble in theirs. The devil's saints have ministers, membership, music, a message, and a mission, just like the Lord's churches do.

THEY GIVE IN CHURCHES

The devil also knows that God's people are supposed to be a GIVING people. They not only should give tithes (10% of their income), but offerings as well. When this is done by a majority of the people in a local church, the church will nearly always find its needs being met. Knowing this, the devil leads his people to give. They not only pay the bills, but they have money left over to support missionaries to go to the foreign field with their imitation gospel.

THEY GROW IN NUMBERS

Some of the phenomenal growth of the cults and charismatics is due to either their extensive visitation work and emotional appeal, but they are definitely growing. Mormon churches and JFW Kingdom Halls are popping up not only in every town, but also all across the world. The cults are beating our missionaries to the foreign fields and establishing their counterfeit churches before we can build TRUE churches. More and more missionaries are telling me there is not a solid gospel witness in a particular town on the foreign field. Then they will add, "Of course, there are Mormon churches, Kingdom Halls, and charismatic churches here already."

I hear from pastors on a daily basis who are struggling with small congregations, trying to make ends meet, and endeavoring to keep the doors open so their community can hear a clear gospel witness. Meanwhile, just down the road from them will be a growing, vibrant Satanic church. Oh, it won't have Satan's name on it, because it's an imitation of the real thing. But it is just as much a Satanic church as the imitation synagogue at Smyrna was in reality a synagogue of the devil:

> **Revelation 2:9 I know thy works, and tribulation, and poverty, (but thou art rich) and I know the blasphemy of them which say they are Jews, and are not, but are the synagogue of Satan.**

Some of the fastest-growing, largest assemblies in the country are those of the devil's counterfeit churches.

In conclusion, the devil's saints appear to be children of God; they act like children of God; they assemble like children of God, but

THEY ARE NOT CHILDREN OF GOD

The religious leaders of Jesus' day were the devil's imitation saints. They claimed to have God as their father. They claimed to be God's people, and they accused Jesus of having a devil. However, the Lord fearlessly spoke the truth to them:

> **John 8:41-44 Ye do the deeds of your father. Then said they to him, We be not born of fornication; we have one Father, even God. 42 Jesus said unto them, If God were your Father, ye would love me: for I proceeded forth and came from God; neither came I of myself, but he sent me. 43 Why do ye not understand my speech? even because ye cannot hear my word. 44 Ye are of your father the devil, and the lusts of your father ye will do. He was a murderer from the beginning, and abode not in the truth, because there is no truth in him. When he speaketh a lie, he speaketh of his own: for he is a liar, and the father of it.**

The devil's saints have **NO TRUE BELIEF IN THE GOSPEL**. They have believed another gospel, which is not another, but is a perversion of the gospel of Christ. The gospel which saves is that of 1 Cor. 15:1-4, which states how that Christ died for our sins according to the scriptures, was buried, and that He rose again the third day according to the scriptures.

There are just two types of people in this world, before God: those who are trusting in Christ and that saving gospel of His atoning work to get them to heaven, and those who aren't. Of these two groups, the Bible says:

> **John 3:18 He that believeth on him is not condemned: but he that believeth not is condemned already, because he hath not believed in the name of the only begotten Son of God.**

> **John 3:36 He that believeth on the Son hath everlasting life: and he that believeth not the Son shall not see life; but the wrath of God abideth on him.**

There are people who know the facts of the gospel, but they have never trusted Christ and His gospel for salvation. The devil's saints are not depending on what Jesus Christ did on the cross to save them. Invariably, they are trusting in one or more of a number of other things:

- Baptism
- Repenting
- Walking an aisle in church
- Committing themselves to live right
- Saying "the sinner's prayer"
- An emotional experience
- A vision
- Financial prosperity
- Good deeds
- Being in the right church
- Showing evidence of salvation
- Membership in a lodge
- Keeping the commandments
- Obeying the Golden Rule
- Not killing anyone

Second, the devil's saints have **NO TRUE BIRTH BY THE SPIRIT OF GOD**. They have made the profession of becoming Christians, but nothing really happened on the inside. A preacher friend of mine brought a message on this subject titled, "Changing the Name, but Staying the Same."

These people are still in the family of Satan. They are not children of God. They can be more accurately described as "children of HELL." At least, that's the way our Lord referred to them in:

> **Matthew 23:15   Woe unto you, scribes and Pharisees, hypocrites! for ye compass sea and land to make one proselyte, and when he is made, ye make him twofold more the child of hell than yourselves.**

It was a RELIGIOUS leader to whom the Lord Jesus spoke those famous words:

> **John 3:7   Marvel not that I said unto thee, Ye must be born again.**

These people, the devil's imitation saints, do not have the Spirit of God. Many of them major on the Spirit of the Lord in their "ministries," but they don't even know Him. Their actions and activities, while similar to those produced under the influence of God's Holy Ghost, are almost completely contrary to God's Spirit. They are in error about holiness, about music, about salvation, about the baptism by the Spirit, about the gifts of the Spirit, about women preachers and teachers, about women speaking in church, about decency and order in church services, and a host of other things with regard to the doctrines of the Spirit. Their errors are due to the fact that they are unable to discern the truth of the word of God, because they don't have the Spirit of God. The Bible says:

1 Corinthians 2:14 But the natural man receiveth not the things of the Spirit of God: for they are foolishness unto him: neither can he know them, because they are spiritually discerned.

These people do not have the Spirit, so they do not have the ability to understand the teachings of the Bible about the Holy Spirit. The fact that they do not have the Holy Spirit also bears witness to the fact that they are NOT God's children. They are NOT God's sheep. They are NOT God's wheat. They are NOT God's SAINTS. They are IMITATION SAINTS.

Romans 8:9 But ye are not in the flesh, but in the Spirit, if so be that the Spirit of God dwell in you. Now if any man have not the Spirit of Christ, he is none of his.

Third and finally, the devil's saints have **NO TRUE BELONGING TO THE LORD** -- THEY ARE NOT HIS. There are a lot of "illegitimate children of God" walking around today, masquerading as Christians. They are illegitimate in that they claim God as their Father when He is not their Father. These people will not be revealed as Satan's people until the Great White Throne Judgment (Rev. 20:11-15), but God knows who they are.

2 Timothy 2:19 Nevertheless the foundation of God standeth sure, having this seal, The Lord knoweth them that are his. And, Let every one that nameth the name of Christ depart from iniquity.

Until that time, it is dangerous for us who are saved to assume that another person is truly saved. You can know that YOU are saved, according to 1 John 5:13. Everyone else you know, however, may be a little more difficult to pin down. This is because of the unusual power that the devil has to produce IMITATION SAINTS.

CHAPTER 5

IMITATION SCRIPTURES

2 Corinthians 2:10-17 To whom ye forgive any thing, I forgive also: for if I forgave any thing, to whom I forgave it, for your sakes forgave I it in the person of Christ; 11 Lest Satan should get an advantage of us: for we are not ignorant of his devices. 12 Furthermore, when I came to Troas to preach Christ's gospel, and a door was opened unto me of the Lord, 13 I had no rest in my spirit, because I found not Titus my brother: but taking my leave of them, I went from thence into Macedonia. 14 Now thanks be unto God, which always causeth us to triumph in Christ, and maketh manifest the savour of his knowledge by us in every place. 15 For we are unto God a sweet savour of Christ, in them that are saved, and in them that perish: 16 To the one we are the savour of death unto death; and to the other the savour of life unto life. And who is sufficient for these things? 17 For we are not as many, which corrupt the word of God: but as of sincerity, but as of God, in the sight of God speak we in Christ.

I decided to print out the entire context of the verse I want to emphasize in this chapter, due to the fact that in the passage the Bible warns us lest Satan should get an advantage of us, for we are not ignorant of his devices. The most obvious reference in the context is to the temptation to be unforgiving. If we cannot forgive someone who has repented, we are setting ourselves up to be defeated by Satan. ALSO in the context, however, is found a reference in verse 17 to "many, which corrupt the word of God":

2 Corinthians 2:17 For we are not as many, which corrupt the word of God: but as of sincerity, but as of God, in the sight of God speak we in Christ.

The reason why so "many" were corrupting the word of God in Paul's day was that the devil was just making another of his many attempts "to be like the most High." He was producing COUNTERFEITS. He was making IMITATIONS of the things of God. As pointed out in previous chapters, that is his great desire. His favorite songs are, "O To Be Like Thee," and "I Would Be Like Jesus." He has copied everything that God is and has. However, since he is a wicked creature as well as an inferior creature, he is unable to COPY the things of God without CORRUPTING the things of God. One of the devil's projects has been to produce:

IMITATION SCRIPTURES

There is one sense in that the scriptures CANNOT be corrupted, for it is written,

1 Peter 1:23   Being born again, not of corruptible seed, but of incorruptible, by the word of God, which liveth and abideth for ever.

The word of God is incorruptible seed. Therefore, it cannot truly be corrupted. The word of God is perfect and will always be around.

However, our text above said that in Paul's day MANY were CORRUPTING the word of God. The only way that could be done is to produce a COUNTERFEIT. Satan has produced IMITATION SCRIPTURES, "scriptures like those of the most High," in which he has added to, subtracted from, and changed the words of the Lord!

Should it surprise us that the devil would have such an envy of God's word? After all, the word of God is highly exalted by the Lord, so much so that the Bible describes it this way:

Psalms 138:2   I will worship toward thy holy temple, and praise thy name for thy lovingkindness and for thy truth: for thou hast magnified thy word above all thy name.

God has magnified His WORD above all His NAME!!! Since the name of Jesus Christ is HIGHER than any name (Phil. 2:9), then the word of God has a lofty position, indeed! The devil, of course, envies the high things of the Lord, as is seen in Isa. 14:12-14, and that includes God's word. It appears to irritate the devil to no end to find that some people accept God's word, admire God's word, adapt to God's word, and appreciate God's word.

If you go down to your local Christian bookstore and ask for a copy of the Bible, they will ask you, "Which Bible would you like?" You might reply,

"I would like a copy of the HOLY Bible," if you didn't know any better. The truth is, new converts DON'T know any better! If you have just gotten saved, you don't know that when you go to the store to buy a Bible that you will have to choose between the KJV, NIV, ESV, RSV, NASB, TEV, TLB, RSVP, and XYZ! You just figure you can ask for "the Bible," and BUY one! That's not possible, however, and the main personality behind the dilemma is SATAN.

Perhaps you have had a problem buying a Bible. For instance, many Christians have heard their pastor recommend a Scofield Reference Bible. That's just a King James Bible with a lot of footnotes and chain references in it. However, unknown to them, there has ALSO been produced a revision called the New Scofield Reference Bible. This edition actually made word changes IN THE TEXT. Changing words in the text disqualified it from being called the King James Version, but it still bore the name on its title page. Sneaky, huh? As a young man, I bought one, a New Scofield, with the most expensive binding they offered, hand-grained Morocco leather. Do you know where it is today? It's on a shelf in my library, gathering dust. I never use it, except to show people what's wrong with it. At the time I bought it, I didn't know anything about the Bible version issue, but I felt the New Scofield must be safe because it said "King James Version" on it. I didn't know that the publishers LIED.

I'll just point out four things in this chapter about the Devil's "bibles." Some people won't appreciate my referring to the one they just received from their "Bible of the Month" Club as "Satan's Bible," but I'm not writing this to make everyone HAPPY; I'm writing to make everyone INFORMED. If you think my wording is harsh, perhaps you will change your mind by the time you have completed reading this chapter.

This chapter is of the utmost importance. It's vital that you get a hold of this. I think one of the most important subjects in the word of God is AUTHORITY. It's no coincidence that the King James Bible, which is GOD'S Bible for today, is also called The Authorized Version. It has AUTHORITY, not the authority of the throne of England, but the authority of the throne of heaven, brother. The devil hates authority, as do his minions. You need an authority for your life. If you don't have an authority on the subject of salvation, for instance, you don't know for CERTAIN how to be SAVED.

Romans 10:17 So then faith cometh by hearing, and hearing by the word of God.

How are we saved? Answer: By grace through faith (Eph. 2:8,9). Where does faith come from? Answer: Hearing. Where does hearing come from? Answer: The word of God! (Rom. 10:17) How do we even know what the GOSPEL is? We go to the SCRIPTURES. Notice the way the gospel is described in 1 Cor. 15; it is "according to the scriptures"!

1 Corinthians 15:3-4 For I delivered unto you first of all that which I also received, how that Christ died for our sins according to the scriptures; 4 And that he was buried, and that he rose again the third day according to the scriptures:

What makes the sacrificial death, burial, and resurrection of the Lord Jesus Christ so significant? Answer: It was "according to the scriptures." The Old Testament prophesied what would happen, and Jesus fulfilled those prophecies.

The scriptures are so important that God wrote them down so you could know the CERTAINTY of the WORDS of truth. The Bible says in:

Proverbs 22:20-21 Have not I written to thee excellent things in counsels and knowledge, 21 That I might make thee know the certainty of the words of truth; that thou mightest answer the words of truth to them that send unto thee?

The above verses make it obvious that God has WRITTEN down His words so we can know the CERTAINTY of the WORDS of TRUTH, not just the message, not just the principles, but the WORDS. The purpose of this is so that the believer will have an absolute authority that he might be able to "answer the words of truth to them that send unto" him.

The first thing I want to say about the subject is

SATAN'S IMITATION SCRIPTURES RESEMBLE THE REAL THING

I can understand the problem that a new convert or an unsaved person has with trying to go into a bookstore and tell the difference between God's Bible and Satan's bibles. They look so much alike! If he's like me, his eye will be caught by the sign over the "Bargain Table," where he will find books and Bibles marked 25% - 75% off. So WHAT -- if the cover says

NEW Scofield Reference Bible? So WHAT -- if the thing is called a NEW King James? What difference does it make when you are ignorant and just don't know any better? After all, you're saving money!

When I bought my New Scofield in early 1972, I didn't know anything about Bible translations. I just knew that an "old" Christian man (he was around 40 back then) had recommended it to me and told me that I couldn't beat the morocco binding for the price (it was sold at a discount). If I were tempted to get bitter about anything I can remember doing as a Christian, I would get bitter about wasting my money on the binding of that New Scofield Reference Bible. There it sits in my library. It has the best binding of any of nearly 1,500 books. As far as I'm concerned, the book isn't worth the paper it was printed on.

By the way, I have dozens of translations. I haven't paid full price for any of them, though. Most of them I picked up at flea markets, Salvation Army stores, and yard sales for 50 cents or a dollar. Several were donated to me, some by people who discovered how perverse the translations were.

I think it is up to preachers to let people know, and help them understand the difference between the things of God and the counterfeits of Satan. The Bible says of the Old Testament priests:

> **Ezekiel 44:23 And they shall teach my people the difference between the holy and profane, and cause them to discern between the unclean and the clean.**

This verse impressed me so much that I titled a sermon on the Bible version issue, "The Holy and the Profane." God's men ought to teach God's people the difference between GOD'S Bibles and Satan's IMITATION SCRIPTURES. I've tried to do that. I've taught lessons on the subject. I teach an entire course on the subject in our Bible Institute. We have put them out in lesson plan format. I have written a short booklet on the subject.

I've brought the Devil's bibles into the pulpit, showed where they were wrong, and thrown some of them across the platform and others of them into the baptistry. If God's men don't do this, many people won't know the difference.

Satan's counterfeit scriptures resemble God's word **IN SIGHT**. A few of the unique perversions, such as The Living Bible and the New World Translation, have had distinctive covers with regard to color, binding, and engraving, but many of the new perversions of scripture have been designed to look exactly like a King James Bible. Unless you look closely, you can't tell if a person has one of the devil's bibles or the true word of God in his hands.

They also resemble God's word IN SOUND. No, they're not exactly the same. And, yes, some of them are very, very different, such as the Amplified, the Living Bible, and some others. But, by and large, the perversions of scripture have a lot of the King James Bible in them. Someone who is a Bible-believer and who has spent a good bit of time in the battle on this issue will recognize a scripture perversion in a moment, but that's not true of John E. Average.

By the way, no one reads anything other than a King James Bible from my pulpit. Some people have lied and said that I won't allow anyone to attend our church services if they come in with another version. That's not true. You can bring any version you like to church. You just won't use it to teach Sunday School or preach from my pulpit unless it is a King James 1611 Authorized Version. If you hear someone read from our pulpit and it doesn't match your King James Bible, don't get shook up. We don't have a Bible corrector in the pulpit; we just have a man who can't read. Some preachers' eyes fail them when they're trying to read the scriptures.

You may have to listen to these other versions for a while until you hear a glaring change. For instance, the RSV was pretty popular when it first came out, and in places it didn't sound that much different from the Authorized Version. But when you get to a place like Job 6:6, all of a sudden you realize that something is really going on here! The King James Bible says in:

> **Job 6:6 Can that which is unsavoury be eaten without salt? or is there any taste in the white of an egg?**

In the preface to the RSV, the publishers wrote, "Yet the King James Version has grave defects ... so many and so serious as to call for revision of the English translation." I suppose the above verse is one example of such grave defects, for the RSV changes "is there any taste in the white of an egg?" to "is there any taste in the slime of the purslane?" What? That is supposed to be an IMPROVEMENT?

Concerning the 1611 Authorized Version, occasionally an idiot will vehemently protest that the current KJV is in actuality a 1769, not a 1611. That's ridiculous. It's a deliberate effort to kill the believer's confidence in the King James Bible. "After all," the idiot says, "you don't really have the 1611 King James. It's been revised, and yours is the 1769 edition. The NEW King James is just another revision in that line."

Excuse me for calling your college professor an idiot. In this case, he is probably not as much of an idiot as he is a devil-filled LIAR. The King James Version IS the 1611 King James Version, and the New King James Version is something else. I have on my table here a copy of the Revised Standard Version of 1952. On the title page it says, "The Holy Bible Containing The Old and New Testaments, Revised Standard Version, Translated from the Original Languages, Being the Version Set Forth A.D. 1611, Revised A.D. 1881-1885 and A.D. 1901, Compared with the Most Ancient Authorities and Revised A.D. 1946-1952, Second Edition of the New Testament A.D. 1971." The RSV translators and publishers knew their competition; it was the A.V. 1611, not 1769. Opponents of the A.V. 1611 today try to get rid of their opposition by trying to pretend it doesn't exist.

The devil's scriptures resemble the word of God **IN SUCCESS** -- at least for a while. What I mean by that is that, with the aid of Madison Avenue advertising campaigns and endorsements by folks like Billy Graham and Jerry Falwell each of the new "bibles" sells like hotcakes ... for a decade or so. Then they begin to run out of energy. The Revised Version of 1881, which came out against the King James, was "the cat's meow" for a while. Now nobody uses it. An American edition was produced, the American Standard Version of 1901. Nobody has a copy today. It died.

More versions were produced, each one claiming to be as good as the King James Version, only better. The Good News for Modern Man was the popular new thing in the early 70's, but who uses it now? The Living Bible, even with the continued endorsements of Graham and Falwell, has to continually go through revisions and remodeling in order to survive. The New American Standard Bible was published to try to keep the old American Standard Version of 1901 alive. It has about breathed its last. The New International Version is really no different than the NASB. Do you think the NEW King James Version is really any different or better than the King James II Version of 1971? No, there's just better promotion and packaging.

Don't be surprised when the new one comes off the press. Take a good look at it, because unless it gets continued promotion from prominent individuals and organizations, it won't last long. Even as Aaron's rod swallowed up the rods of the magicians of Egypt, the King James Bible, the King of the Books, eats the new versions up and spits them out.

SATAN'S IMITATION SCRIPTURES RECEIVE PRAISE FROM THE RELIGIOUS CROWD

One of the testimonies to the fact that the King James Bible is the word of God is that the world always flocks to the new versions and praises them to high heaven. When I say, "the world," I am referring to the RELIGIOUS world, those who claim to have some interest in the word of God.

> **Luke 16:15 And he said unto them, Ye are they which justify yourselves before men; but God knoweth your hearts: for that which is highly esteemed among men is abomination in the sight of God.**

Be careful. When you find that the world in general praises something in the realm of religion, that thing that is being praised is probably as wicked as the devil.

THE UNSAVED RELIGIOUS CROWD praises Satan's imitation scriptures. When you find unsaved people who claim to be religious, yet they deny the fundamentals of the faith, you have found people who are NOT going to choose the King James Version for their choice of Bibles. They are generally going to go for something that has already given up the ghost or is close to it. An example would be the Revised Standard Version. You won't find ANYONE using the RSV today. If you do find someone reading an RSV, it is almost ALWAYS an unsaved person.

THE UNGODLY RELIGIOUS CROWD praises Satan's imitation scriptures. I'm talking about people who are not separated from sin and wickedness. These people are those who think you're a fit representative of Jesus Christ if you dress like a slob to go visiting for the church. They think it's all right to have loose morals and have an occasional drink of liquor as long as you don't get drunk. Those are the kind of people who carry the Good News Bible in their hip pocket.

I was preaching across the street from a liquor store a number of years ago, and one of these limp-wristed panty-waists of a fellow came up to me with a Good News Bible in his back pocket. He said, "You are not going to win them that way!" Of course, he was referring to the fact that I was preaching hell fire and damnation. I told the shoppers that if they didn't believe on Christ they would "bust hell wide open." I don't see why you can't win them that way. I believe the word of God will work out in the street across from a liquor store just like it will inside a church building. His problem was that he wanted to go into the store and be accepted by that ungodly crowd so he could get a chance to witness without offending anyone. My friend, if you can live in the midst of folks who are living in open rebellion to God without offending them, something is wrong with your Christianity. If you live right in their presence, the wicked will resent you.

The more wicked that a religious person is, the more likely that he is to pick an off-the-wall version, like the Cottonpatch Version or the Weymouth Version or the Charlie Brown Version. A common version, known as a paraphrase, that is a favorite of wicked people is the Living Bible. The fact that Billy Graham and Jerry Falwell also liked that perversion of scripture is not a note in its favor.

THE UNBELIEVING RELIGIOUS CROWD praises Satan's imitation scriptures. I use the term, "unbelieving," here not just as a reference to unsaved people, but to ANYONE who doesn't believe ALL of the Bible. Many saved people have the word of God (King James Bible) right in front of their faces, but they won't accept it. They're fools. Notice how the Lord Jesus dealt with such unbelieving believers:

> **Luke 24:25 Then he said unto them, O fools, and slow of heart to believe all that the prophets have spoken:**

Jesus wasn't talking to the devil's children when He said those words. He was calling His OWN disciples fools, for not believing ALL that the prophets have spoken. The apostle Paul was used to being called names by lost people. He said,

> **Acts 24:14 But this I confess unto thee, that after the way which they call heresy, so worship I the God of my fathers, believing all things which are written in the law and in the prophets:**

So, if you don't mind, I'll join the Lord in calling people who don't believe everything God wrote "fools," and I am willing to align myself with Paul in that I'm willing to be called a heretic because I believe all things which ARE written (not WERE written) in the law and in the prophets in my Bible. Sometimes a fool will call the Bible-believing body of Christ "The King James Cult." That's okay; I can handle being called names by an idiot. Say I'm in a cult if you want to; if it is a cult, it is made up of fundamental, Bible-believing Christians.

SATAN'S IMITATION SCRIPTURES ROB THE BELIEVER OF RELIABILITY

Satan wants to take out of your hand the one reliable thing upon which you can lay your hand! You can't rely on this preacher. I can't rely on you. We can ALL rely, however, on the BIBLE! The one thing in this world you can put your hands on that you know will never fail you is this BOOK. The devil's bibles are designed to promote such doubt about the inerrancy of ANY available Bible, that they remove the believer's final, absolute authority. This has been the devil's work since the beginning. When he questioned the word of God before Eve and asked, "Yea, hath God said ...?" (Gen. 3:1), he was just setting the stage for a habit that he would exhibit until he is thrown into the lake of fire to burn for all eternity.

The final authority in my church is not me. It is not any other pastor. It certainly is not the congregation or any part of the congregation. The final authority in our church is THE WORD OF GOD. It is a tremendous blessing to pastor a church where the Bible is the ruling document. Nothing overshadows it. My longest pastorate was at Gospel Light Baptist Church in Albany, Georgia. I served there from 1986 to 2012, 26 years. For the entire time that I was there, the Constitution and By-laws of that church was the King James Bible. The Articles of Faith were the King James Bible. The Church Covenant was simply the King James Bible. The Articles of Incorporation (we had none) was the King James Bible.

You say, "How do you solve problems and settle arguments in your church?" That's easy. We do it with prayer and the word of God (the King James Bible)! Thank GOD for a congregation that accepts the King James Bible as GOD'S WORD!

> **1 Thessalonians 2:13 For this cause also thank we God without ceasing, because, when ye received the word of God which ye heard of us, ye received it not as the word of men, but as it is in truth, the word of God, which effectually worketh also in you that believe.**

When you teach or preach something from the word of God that a modern man does not agree with or does not like, he will say, "Well, that book you're using is just a translation." He sits in judgment on the word of God instead of letting the word of God sit in judgment on him.

The devil is successful when he can get someone to doubt that the word of God is available in an inerrant form ANYWHERE. Those people who don't like the King James Version Bible believers don't disagree with us because they think the NASB is the infallible word. They don't believe that ANY Bible that you can put your hands on today is infallible! People who use the NIV don't believe it's perfect. They bitterly resent the fact that we believe that our King James Bible is perfect!

This is the same type of animosity that unsaved religious people have toward us Christians about our "know-so" salvation. They don't know that they are saved and going to heaven, so they really get bitter about the fact that WE DO. Bible-rejecting religionists don't have a Bible that they believe, so they can't STAND the fact that we have a Bible that WE DO believe!

Satan's imitation scriptures rob the believer of his absolute, final authority **FOR HIS BELIEFS**. By putting out a number of conflicting authorities, the devil endeavors to remove from the mind of the individual the need to submit to any one final authority, particularly the word of God. If no intact, inerrant copy of the word of God exists, then no one can be absolutely certain that his beliefs are any better or more reliable than those of anyone else. On the other hand, a Bible believer is more apt to have the attitude expressed below:

Romans 3:4 God forbid: yea, let God be true, but every man a liar; as it is written, That thou mightest be justified in thy sayings, and mightest overcome when thou art judged.

Additionally, Satan's imitation scriptures rob the believer of his absolute, final authority **FOR HIS BEHAVIOR**. The Lord will deal with your heart from the word of God about how to live. The Bible contains many rules for living -- rules, not suggestions. You can say what you want to about grace versus law. You will find rules for "thou shalt" and "thou shalt not" throughout the New Testament as well as the Old. With the exception of the commandment about the sabbath day, which was a peculiar thing, a sign, between God and Israel, all of the 10 commandments given to Moses are repeated time and again in the New Testament. The devil wants to remove the authority of the Bible from the mind of a person so he won't feel so badly when a clear commandment is given in scripture about the individual's behavior.

When the devil tried to influence the behavior of the Lord Jesus Christ, the Savior replied with the authority of the word of God:

Luke 4:4 And Jesus answered him, saying, It is written, That man shall not live by bread alone, but by every word of God.

If the devil can remove that authority from the believer, he has removed the believer's ability to dogmatically declare some behavior to be holy and other behavior to be wicked.

Satan's imitation scriptures rob the believer of his absolute, final authority **FOR HIS BATTLES**. Thoughtful Christians have observed that in the temptation of the Lord by Satan, the Son of God met the foe with scripture quotations. "It is written ..." "It is written ..." "It is written ..." should be the way that the believer fights his battles today. Our battles are of a spiritual nature; therefore we need spiritual weapons. The Bible lays out a description of the spiritual armor that a Christian should wear in his daily life. Included in the list is the following admonition:

Ephesians 6:17 And take the helmet of salvation, and the sword of the Spirit, which is the word of God:

If the devil can talk you out of your faith in the word of God by putting out so many versions on the market that you begin to feel that none of them is authoritative, he has ripped your sword out of your hand. The sword of the Spirit is the one and only offensive weapon in the list in Ephesians 6. If Satan persuades you to start using one of the new versions, like the New International Version or the New King James Version, he has removed the sword of the Spirit, and placed a rubber knife in your hand.

Don't let it happen! Follow the example of Eleazar, in his battle against the Philistines:

2 Samuel 23:10 He arose, and smote the Philistines until his hand was weary, and his hand clave unto the sword: and the LORD wrought a great victory that day; and the people returned after him only to spoil.

I've seen pro-gun bumper stickers which said something like, "They Can Have My Gun When They Pry My Cold Dead Fingers Off It." Well, I feel the same way about the King James Bible. The devil can continue to put out his "scriptures like those of the most High." I'll just stick with the REAL THING, thank you.

Finally ...

SATAN'S IMITATION SCRIPTURES REMOVE GREAT REALITIES OF THE FAITH

One of the common defenses of Satan's bibles is that none of the changes affect any doctrines of the Bible. That is said to give you the idea that the only thing changed in the new bibles was the removal of "thee" and "thou." The truth is, there are a number of changes made, common to nearly all of the new bibles, in select places, which affect IMPORTANT doctrines. I'm going to take the NWT (the New World Translation of the Jehovah's False Witnesses), the RSV (Revised Standard Version), the NASB (New American Standard Bible), the NIV (New International Version), and the ESV (English Standard Version), to show you that there is a little more involved in this business than changing "thee" to "you." You will see a common thread of changes affecting essential doctrines in the following verses. These changes are common to MOST of the new versions. I've just picked these four out as samples of the devil's IMITATION SCRIPTURES.

Let me start with a change in the Old Testament that deliberately removes a pre-incarnate appearance of the Lord Jesus Christ. First, reading from the King James Bible, we find:

Daniel 3:25 He answered and said, Lo, I see four men loose, walking in the midst of the fire, and they have no hurt; and the form of the fourth is like the Son of God.

In the above verse, Jesus Christ made an Old Testament appearance. Readers of the King James Bible know who the fourth man in the fire was. We have taught our little children from this passage that if you will go through the fire for the Lord Jesus Christ, He will be in the fire for you.

I ran into one of my friends whom I had not seen for years and years. He said, "I'm ready to take you to task over the issue of the King James Bible."

"Okay," I said. "By the way, which Bible are you using?" You might as well ask these folks which Bible that they USE, rather than which one that they BELIEVE, because these Bible-rejecting fools don't BELIEVE ANY Bible. I'm not thrilled about people who USE the King James Bible, unless they also BELIEVE the King James Bible. Friend, BELIEVE what you USE, and USE what you BELIEVE.

He said, "I'm using the New Scofield."

"Good," I replied. "Before we get into our discussion, let me ask you a question. Who was the fourth man in the fire with the three Hebrew children in the book of Daniel?"

"That was Jesus," he said.

"How do you know that?" I asked.

He said, "It's in the Bible."

"It's in MINE," I said. "IT'S NOT IN YOURS."

He had not read his New Scofield enough to find that out, and he was shocked when he turned to it. The New Scofield reads just like the Jehovah's Witness Bible in Dan. 3:25. The New World Translation changes "the Son of God" to "a son of the gods." That sounds pagan, doesn't it? You can't tell that's Jesus in the fire, from the JFW Bible. You say, "Well, Preacher, I don't believe in using that cult Bible." Well, the New Scofield is no better on that great verse. I want you to know there is not a bit of difference on this verse between the Satanic JFW Bible and the new versions used by "conservatives." The Revised Standard Version reads, "a son of the gods." Isn't it amazing that the RSV is just like the Jehovah's Witness perversion? The New American Standard Bible, used by many fundamentalists until the NIV came out, says, "a son of the gods." Well, the new "baby" of conservatives, the NIV, says exactly the same thing: "a son of the gods." The ESV says, "a son of the gods." The NSRB, the RSV, the NASB, the NIV, and the ESV are NO BETTER than the Jehovah's Witnesses bible on this verse! The JFW's believe Jesus was a son of the gods; Christians don't. We believe that He is the Son of God! And all of God's people said ... "AMEN!"

Let's look at another one in the King James Bible. Here is another Old Testament prophecy that proclaims the deity of Christ and His eternal nature:

> **Micah 5:2 But thou, Bethlehem Ephratah, though thou be little among the thousands of Judah, yet out of thee shall he come forth unto me that is to be ruler in Israel; whose goings forth have been from of old, from everlasting.**

This great prophetic verse, as it reads in your KJV, shows the eternal nature of the Lord Jesus Christ. He had no beginning, and He has no ending. Rather, He IS the beginning, and He IS the ending. He has no origin. His goings forth have been from everlasting. The JFW's (Jehovah's False Witnesses), of course, do not believe that. They believe that Jesus was created, and that He had an origin. Therefore, it is no great surprise that their Bible, the NWT, changes "goings forth" to "origins." Beloved, when you give Jesus an origin (other than that of physical birth), you are turning Jesus into a creature rather than the Creator, and that is heresy. Jesus HAD no origin.

Checking the RSV, it reads, "whose origin." Isn't it amazing that the RSV reads almost exactly the same as the cult JFW bible on a verse that has to do with the eternal nature of our Lord and Savior Jesus Christ? Well, the NASB isn't quite as bad. It keeps the words "goings forth," but rather than say, "whose goings forth have been from of old, from everlasting," it says, "whose goings forth are from long ago, from the days of eternity." Then the NIV, when we check it, says, "whose origins are from of old, from ancient times." On this verse, the NIV is as bad as the JFW's bible, and it's WORSE than the NASB. The New International Version is not worth the paper it's printed on! I have one, because it was GIVEN to me. I wouldn't pay more than 50 cents for it, a dollar TOPS. The ESV says, "whose coming forth is from of old, from ancient days." ... anything but "from everlasting"!

Let's look at another Old Testament verse. In the King James Bible we have another prophecy of Jesus Christ, this time His crucifixion, in:

Zechariah 13:6 And one shall say unto him, What are these wounds in thine hands? Then he shall answer, Those with which I was wounded in the house of my friends.

This prophecy about the Lord Jesus Christ has been obscured in many of the new bibles. The wounds in His hands were, of course, identifying marks which convinced doubting Thomas. He will show those wounds to Israel when He returns to earth at the Second Advent. The JFW bible, the NWT, says, "... what are these wounds on your person between your hands? And he will have to say, Those with which I was struck in the house of my intense lovers." Intense lovers? That sounds like a pretty "queer" translation, if you ask me. The RSV says, "... what are these wounds on your back?" Your BACK? Thomas didn't ask to see the Lord's back. The NASB says, "... what are these wounds between your arms?" The NIV, one of the biggest pieces of corruption in my generation, says, "...what are these wounds on your body?" And the ESV reads like the RSV, saying, "What are these wounds on your back?" These PERversions are all CORRUPT.

Oh, yes! These changes in the new versions affect more than just "archaic language." They change more than just "thee" and "thou."

Let's move on to the New Testament. One of the truths the Devil hates is the virgin birth, which is closely associated with the deity of Jesus Christ. We're not talking about an "incidental." We're talking about a "fundamental." The King James Bible says in:

> **Luke 2:33   And Joseph and his mother marvelled at those things which were spoken of him.**

The Jehovah's Witnesses do not believe in the deity of Christ. Now I know what you're thinking. You're thinking, "Well, Preacher, surely they didn't remove ALL the references to Christ's deity." You're right. They don't. But rat poison isn't mostly poison; it's mostly food. The small percentage of poison is what gets the rat. The new bibles aren't 100% poison, but they are more deadly than any pesticide known to man.

The King James Bible is very precise here, calling Mary the Lord's mother and Joseph just "Joseph." The reason for that is simple. Joseph was NOT the Lord's FATHER. When Mary found the 12-year-old Jesus in the temple, she told Him that His father had been looking for him. The Lord's reply to her was, "Wist ye not that I must be about my FATHER'S business?" The NWT, put out by the JFW's, changes "Joseph and his mother" to "its father and mother" and changes "were spoken of him" to "being spoken about it." That's not surprising. After all, the NWT is a CULT's bible. They don't believe in the deity of Christ, and the virgin birth testifies to His deity! The RSV, which is just as much the devil's bible as is the NWT, reads, "his father and his mother." The NASB says, "his father and mother." The NIV says, "the child's father and mother." The ESV says, "his father and mother." Here is another example where the other new PERversions are NO BETTER than the phony-baloney bible of the Jehovah's Witnesses.

Let's look at another change that affects the Bible's declaration about hell. The King James Bible says in:

> **Luke 16:23   And in hell he lift up his eyes, being in torments, and seeth Abraham afar off, and Lazarus in his bosom.**

Nearly all of the cults deny the fact of eternal torment in hell. Therefore, one of the passages of the Bible that they hate the most is Luke 16. First, they attack it by calling it a parable, when the Bible doesn't call it a parable. Then they try to cool off hell by changing the word. Let's look at what Satan's bibles have done to Luke 16:23.

The NWT of the Jehovah's False Witnesses changes "hell" to "hades." We're not surprised that they did that. I wouldn't want the Bible to say "hell" if I thought that I was going there, either! Conservative Christians aren't really surprised that a Jehovah's False Witness translation would try to "cool off" hell. However, a supposedly "Christian" version, the RSV, says "hades," just like the cult translation does. The NASB also says, "hades." Does nobody believe that the rich man went to HELL? As for the NIV, this is one of the few places where the NIV matches the King James rather than the Jehovah's Witnesses bible. The ESV changes "hell" to "Hades."

You know, one of the supposed reasons for these new versions is to put the Bible in a language that today's people can understand. Scoffers say that you have to get special training to understand the King James Bible. Baloney. You don't need special training; you need a special BIRTH by the Spirit of God! These new IMITATION SCRIPTURES change a word that is used by common people (especially unsaved people) in America every hour of every day! Whoever heard of "Hades Angels"? Have you ever been told to go to hades? I haven't.

Let's look at another change. This one affects not only the doctrine of the deity of Christ, but the doctrine of the resurrection of Christ! That is NOT an unimportant doctrine. It is FUNDAMENTAL. The King James Bible says in:

Acts 1:3 To whom also he shewed himself alive after his passion by many infallible proofs, being seen of them forty days, and speaking of the things pertaining to the kingdom of God:

The doctrine of the resurrection of Christ is essential. The proofs of that resurrection, according to the above verse, were "infallible." I love that word, don't you? JFW's are in error on the literal, bodily resurrection of Jesus Christ. That is, they don't believe the gospel of 1 Cor. 15:3,4. Therefore, they are LOST. Their bible, the NWT says, "positive proofs" instead of "infallible proofs." Some translators didn't like that word, "infallible," did they? The RSV says "many proofs," completely omitting the word "infallible." The NASB says, "many convincing proofs." Lots of things are CONVINCING that aren't INFALLIBLE. Many things on television are CONVINCING. Magicians are convincing. The NIV says, "many convincing proofs." The ESV just removes the word "infallible," leaving it as "many proofs."

Let's look at another one. Do you realize that it is required that a person be a believer, that is, born again, saved, headed for heaven, BEFORE getting baptized. That is the clear teaching of the King James Bible in:

Acts 8:37 And Philip said, If thou believest with all thine heart, thou mayest. And he answered and said, I believe that Jesus Christ is the Son of God.

In the previous verse the new convert asked Philip what would hinder him from getting baptized. Verse 37 records Philip's answer. The requirement that a person must meet before he can be baptized is that he must be saved. That is, he must have believed on the Lord Jesus first BEFORE he can be baptized. However, the NWT omits verse 37, leaving the question unanswered. The RSV leaves it out. My copy of the NASB has the verse in brackets, with a note saying the verse should be left out. The NIV I have leaves it out, just like the NWT and the RSV did. So does the ESV.

Here is another one. Apparently, those who produced the IMITATION SCRIPTURES have a problem with a New Testament Bible verse that commands people to tell the truth! We read in the King James Bible in:

Romans 13:9 For this, Thou shalt not commit adultery, Thou shalt not kill, Thou shalt not steal, Thou shalt not bear false witness, Thou shalt not covet; and if there be any other commandment, it is briefly comprehended in this saying, namely, Thou shalt love thy neighbour as thyself.

With this verse, we judge the MOTIVES of the people putting out the new "bibles". You say, "You're judging?" Absolutely. Of the commandments in this verse, there is ONE of them which is completely LEFT OUT of the NWT, the RSV, the NASB, the NIV, the ESV, and nearly all of the REST of Satan's bibles. Do you have to guess which one it is? They removed, "Thou shalt not bear false witness"! Now, why would they do that? Is it important to tell the truth? Is it archaic to tell the truth? Why did these versions leave that out?

Here is another one. In your King James Bible you will find this verse:

Colossians 1:14 In whom we have redemption through his blood, even the forgiveness of sins:

People say that the fundamentals of the faith are not affected in the changes made by the new versions. Oh, is that so? Then why did the NWT leave out the words, "through his blood" in Col. 1:14? Why did the RSV omit the words? Ditto the NASB, the NIV, and the ESV? Answer: they all are related. These IMITATION SCRIPTURES were birthed in HELL. The blood atonement is not an "incidental." It is a FUNDAMENTAL.

Here is a shocking change. In the King James Bible, the Lord said in:

> **Luke 4:4 And Jesus answered him, saying, It is written, That man shall not live by bread alone, but by every word of God.**

Some folks, including the Devil, think that we are NOT to live by "every word." They try to tell us that "every word" is not important. Would you believe that the NWT, the RSV, the NASB, the NIV, and the ESV ALL omit the words, "but by every word of God"? That's right. In each of those "perversions" of scripture, the verse ends with "alone." That wasn't done because you can't understand the "archaic" words, "but by every word of God." The DEVIL was behind that change!

Let's look at one more, and we'll close out this chapter. In the King James Bible, we read in:

> **1 Thessalonians 1:6 And ye became followers of us, and of the Lord, having received the word in much affliction, with joy of the Holy Ghost.**

The NWT changes "followers" to "imitators." That's because the NWT is an imitation bible. The RSV reads, "imitators." Do you care to guess what the NASB, the NIV, and the ESV say here? Do you have to guess?

This is just the tip of the iceberg. These IMITATION SCRIPTURES are full of corruptions, and there are more of these counterfeits being published every year or so.

Beware of Satan's IMITATION SCRIPTURES!

CHAPTER 6

IMITATION SHEPHERDS

2 Corinthians 11:14-15 And no marvel; for Satan himself is transformed into an angel of light. 15 Therefore it is no great thing if his ministers also be transformed as the ministers of righteousness; whose end shall be according to their works.

In his desire "to be like the most High," the Devil has imitated the ambassadors whom the Lord uses to declare His precepts and to direct His people. The devil's shepherds are not true shepherds. They are hirelings. A hireling wants whatever he can get out of the sheep. He wants to FLEECE the sheep. The Lord Jesus told Peter to FEED the sheep, not FLEECE the sheep. The New Testament principle is that if the shepherd feeds the sheep spiritually, then they can FEED him materially. That is, if he provides their spiritual needs, they are to provide his physical or material needs.

Have you ever run into Satan's counterfeit ministers? Have you ever seen them? Have you ever heard them speak? I have. I've talked to them personally. I have heard them on television and radio. You should beware, because it is possible that the minister whom you hear on radio, see on television, or read through the printed page is just an imitation of a man of God. The devil is out to deceive people by imitating all of the things of God, including God's preachers!

Some men are indeed "called to preach," but they are called by the wrong god! They are called by the wrong spirit! Their calling is not to exalt Jesus Christ; it is to direct people AWAY from Jesus Christ. The devil, of course, is not going to put up a big sign that says, "Worship Satan Here." He knows that people will not react positively to that; his name has too many negative things associated with it. He will say, rather, "Worship GOD." He will, however, direct their attention away from the true God and toward himself.

The Bible speaks of these IMITATION SHEPHERDS as false prophets, who are wolves in sheep's clothing.

> **Matthew 7:15 Beware of false prophets, which come to you in sheep's clothing, but inwardly they are ravening wolves.**

The church at Ephesus was commended for examining and exposing the devil's counterfeit apostles:

> **Revelation 2:2 I know thy works, and thy labour, and thy patience, and how thou canst not bear them which are evil: and thou hast tried them which say they are apostles, and are not, and hast found them liars:**

CONSIDER THE APPEARANCE OF THE DEVIL'S IMITATION SHEPHERDS

> **2 Corinthians 11:13-15 For such are false apostles, deceitful workers, transforming themselves into the apostles of Christ. 14 And no marvel; for Satan himself is transformed into an angel of light. 15 Therefore it is no great thing if his ministers also be transformed as the ministers of righteousness; whose end shall be according to their works.**

I don't believe that the antichrist is going to make his appearance while you and I are on the earth. I don't believe that he will show up, although he may already be living, until after the church has been called up into heaven at the Rapture. When he appears then, he may show up in a "flying saucer". You know, people are truly looking toward outer space right now. They are looking toward the heavens for the answer to life's problems. A number of television shows and movies are built around the theme of aliens visiting from outer space. An unusual amount of interest was sparked as we came to a new millennium.

It could be that the antichrist will be connected with UFOs (Unidentified Flying Objects). If he is, I don't think that he will look like the Lord Jesus Christ REALLY looks, but as people PERCEIVE him to appear. That perception is based upon deceptive misrepresentations of the Lord Jesus Christ promulgated by the devil over the last 20 centuries.

Likewise, the devil's ministers don't look like you would think. They don't glare. They don't smoke (except perhaps some tobacco). They don't carry pitchforks. They aren't dressed in red outfits.

IT IS A PROFESSIONAL APPEARANCE. I believe the devil's ministers, his IMITATION SHEPHERDS, look like your preacher does when he is dressed in his best suit. The devil has read and mastered, "How to Dress for Success." His preachers aren't going to dress like dirty bums. They won't be rude and crude. They will be professional. They know how to carry themselves. They hold their Bibles "just right." They know how to perform weddings and funerals with great dignity and without offending anyone. They know how to behave at the bedside of a hospital patient. They are professionals. The only exception to that would be in "churches" where it is the norm for everyone, including the minister, to dress like a bum.

One of the most professional ministers I have ever heard was the late Garner Ted Armstrong of the Worldwide Church of God. The man was a cult member for as long as I can remember. He was a minister of Satan, although he did not, of course, profess to be such. However, you will be hard pressed to find a more professional radio or television speaker than he was in his prime. I'm telling you, he did it with class. The devil is slick.

IT IS A PLEASING APPEARANCE. In his desire to deceive as many people as possible, I believe that the devil tries to make his ministers as pleasing in their appearance as possible. They aren't rough, tough, crude and rude Rednecks. They're pleasant.

Do you know that the apostle Paul was rude? Look at verse six of our scripture:

> **2 Corinthians 11:6 But though I be rude in speech, yet not in knowledge; but we have been throughly made manifest among you in all things.**

The word, "rude," has to do with BASIC. Most people think of the word as being a reference to mean, obnoxious, and hateful. I don't believe that's what Paul meant. I don't think, however, that he was that careful about being sure that he dressed according to the latest fashions.

I think of John the Baptist. I have an idea that he was a rude sort of fellow. The Bible says he liked to eat locusts and wild honey. In a message about John, I depicted a preacher walking along dipping locusts in honey and chewing them up. You should have seen some of the scowls, frowns, and other unpleasant looks that I got, especially from the little children who thought that was "gross," to think of eating something like a grasshopper! What would you think if I came to church Sunday morning driving a pickup truck and when you came to my window you saw two bowls in the seat -- one containing honey, and the other with locusts?

The devil's ministers won't be found riding in a pickup truck or Jeep. They won't be wearing a pair of boots. They will be careful to appear like people would want their minister to look.

This pleasing appearance is one in which the minister always wears a smile. One of my pastor friends who has his photograph on the Internet got chewed out by a visitor to his website, because the photo didn't show him with a smile. Well, bless your little pea-picking heart!

I think that God's people should be a joyous people. However, do you think that John the Baptist was always smiling? I don't. Some people came to his baptism, and he bellowed at them, "Who hath warned you to flee from the wrath to come?" I don't think that he smiled when he said that. You know, some preachers smile all through their sermons. They grin while they preach on hell. I have an idea that John gritted his teeth, wrinkled his forehead, and turned red in the face when he told those hypocrites to bring forth fruits meet for repentance, and then he might consider talking with them.

I don't think that the Lord Jesus Christ had a pleasing appearance when He cleared the temple. I believe He hollered at that bingo-playing crowd as He turned over their tables, whipped them with a scourge, and scared them out of their wits.

IT IS A PHONY APPEARANCE. Jesus said of the unsaved religious crowd that they were like whitened sepulchres. They were walking crypts. Outside, they were painted and polished. Inside, they were filled with dead men's bones, cobwebs, and creepy, crawly things. Satan's imitation shepherd may be smiling on the outside, but he is frowning on the inside. I know. I have provoked some of the devil's ministers, and their "real" side, the INSIDE, came out!

CONSIDER THE ATTITUDE OF THE DEVIL'S IMITATION SHEPHERDS

> **Romans 16:17-18 Now I beseech you, brethren, mark them which cause divisions and offences contrary to the doctrine which ye have learned; and avoid them. 18 For they that are such serve not our Lord Jesus Christ, but their own belly;**

and by good words and fair speeches deceive the hearts of the simple.

THEY CAUSE DECEPTION. Deception is the devil's business, and his ministers do his business. Therefore, they deceive like he does. Of course, the way that they do it, according to Rom. 16:17-18, is by "good words and fair speeches." They deceive like politicians deceive. They promise everything in the world, and even their negative statements are made to sound positive. The Bible warns us in:

2 Timothy 3:13 But evil men and seducers shall wax worse and worse, deceiving, and being deceived.

They lie to people about salvation, teaching that a person is saved or that he is kept saved by his works. They lie to people about the scriptures, teaching folks that no one can have a Bible that is the infallible word of God from cover to cover. They lie about sin, stating that what was wrong many years ago may be all right today.

THEY CREATE DIVISION (Rom. 16:17-18). Of course, wicked people always accuse the Bible-believing fundamentalists of creating division. The division, however, is caused by the liberals, modernists, and infidels. They try to separate people away from Bible-believing Christianity. The Bible speaks of this device in:

Jude 1:18-19 How that they told you there should be mockers in the last time, who should walk after their own ungodly lusts. 19 These be they who separate themselves, sensual, having not the Spirit.

Notice that the above verse, dealing with "mockers" who "walk after their own ungodly lusts," also says that they "separate themselves." Question: from whom do they separate? the compromising contemporary church movement? No. The Catholics? No. The Promise Keepers? No. They separate themselves from fanatical, right-wing, Bible-believing fundamentalists!

THEY CONTRADICT DOCTRINE. Paul, when talking about the scriptures, said they were given by inspiration of God, and they were profitable for DOCTRINE. As a matter of fact, in the list of four areas in which the scriptures are profitable, DOCTRINE is NUMBER ONE on the list!

2 Timothy 3:16 All scripture is given by inspiration of God, and is profitable for doctrine, for reproof, for correction, for instruction in righteousness:

Doctrine is important. Every Christian ought to be in a local church that teaches sound doctrine. Every preacher should be schooled in the doctrine of the word of God. There are too many of the devil's ministers teaching false doctrine, for the ministers of the Lord to neglect teaching sound doctrine. Paul told Titus that the way a preacher was to overcome the error being promulgated by wicked teachers and preachers was through teaching SOUND DOCTRINE:

Titus 1:9-11 Holding fast the faithful word as he hath been taught, that he may be able by sound doctrine both to exhort and to convince the gainsayers. 10 For there are many unruly and vain talkers and deceivers, specially they of the circumcision: 11 Whose mouths must be stopped, who subvert whole houses, teaching things which they ought not, for filthy lucre's sake.

While some of the devil's IMITATION SHEPHERDS, such as preachers and teachers of Catholicism, Mormonism, and Jehovah's Witnesses, will contradict sound doctrine by teaching heresy, others will contradict sound doctrine simply by avoiding it. They will try to unite people at the expense of doctrine. They will minimize doctrine, and they will teach that doctrine is actually a hindrance to Christian unity.

THEY CIRCULATE DOUBT. It has been said that the devil is just one big question mark. In the garden of Eden, he made his appearance by casting a doubt upon the word of God that Eve had received. When the devil tempted the Lord Jesus Christ, he said to him, "IF thou be the Son of God..." At the crucifixion, the devil's people followed suit. Notice the "if" in:

Matthew 27:39-40 And they that passed by reviled him, wagging their heads, 40 And saying, Thou that destroyest the temple, and buildest it in three days, save thyself. If thou be the Son of God, come down from the cross.

Some people think that one of the healthiest things that a ministerial student learns in seminary is to ask questions. What they mean by that is that he needs to be willing to DOUBT what he has been taught. That is interesting, since Paul said a preacher should HOLD FAST the faithful word "AS he hath been taught" (Tit. 1:9). I want to be open to the word of God, and I want to be open to the truth. I am NOT open, however, to criticism of the Bible!

Some time ago I was involved in correspondence with a college professor at a Baptist graduate school. He used good words and fair speeches, throwing me a compliment here and there. Then, he began to question my Bible and my faith in it. Do you know what I told him? I said, "Look; I recognize your voice. I've heard it before." I then quoted Gen. 3:1:

> **Genesis 3:1 Now the serpent was more subtil than any beast of the field which the LORD God had made. And he said unto the woman, Yea, hath God said, Ye shall not eat of every tree of the garden?**

You say, "Preacher, did you actually call that college professor the devil?" That's right.

The devil's imitation shepherds circulate doubt about the scriptures. They endeavor to place a question mark in the mind of the believer about the word of God. I was saved in 1968. At this date, after reading my Bible through from cover to cover scores of times, as well as reading hundreds of theological works ABOUT the Bible, I want to publicly state that I believe my Bible today more than I did when I first got saved. Yes, I have had it questioned by people who brought alleged contradictions to my attention. Yes, I have read things in the Bible that I did not understand. But, no, I don't doubt the word of God at all.

As a matter of fact, you might say that I have a "bad attitude," when it comes to this subject. When I suspect a fellow is trying to deceive people about the inerrancy of the word of God, I'll jump on him in a minute.

CONSIDER THE APPETITES OF THE DEVIL'S IMITATION SHEPHERDS

> **2 Peter 2:1 But there were false prophets also among the people, even as there shall be false teachers among you, who privily shall bring in damnable heresies, even denying the Lord that bought them, and bring upon themselves swift destruction.**

> **2 Peter 2:14 Having eyes full of adultery, and that cannot cease from sin; beguiling unstable souls: an heart they have exercised with covetous practices; cursed children:**

In this chapter, unsaved false prophets are compared to DOGS (male false prophets) and SOWS (female false prophetesses). Have you ever considered the dietary habits of dogs and swine? Oh, my. Read it in the context:

2 Peter 2:22 But it is happened unto them according to the true proverb, The dog is turned to his own vomit again; and the sow that was washed to her wallowing in the mire.

THEY WANT THE WEALTH. The Bible says that the devil's imitation shepherds exercise their hearts with "covetous practices." One of the imitation shepherds who is the most open along these lines was a fellow who called himself "Reverend Ike." He died in 2009. He made no bones about his covetousness. He was after the MONEY. His ministry was about money. His theme was: "How to Use Your Mind Power to Get What You Want." I'm not misrepresenting him; that's exactly what he preached. He used to come out each month on the radio with a "Mind Power Idea." He used slogans like, "Mind power is green power." "Mind power is MONEY-getting power." He said, "I don't want the pie-in-the-sky bye and bye. I want mine NOW, with a cherry on top!" He appealed to a great segment of the population who desire to get rich without working.

The statement, "Every man has his price," should not be true of God's men. It is sad but true that many preachers will not assume the pastorate of a church without negotiating for their salary, just like a person might do who is applying for a secular job. That's a shame. I don't think that a salary ought to even be a consideration when a man of God is contemplating moving to an area to reach the lost with the gospel of Christ.

I have been pastoring continuously since 1975. Over the years I have pastored at times when the churches were able to take care of my financial needs, and I did not have to do anything else to bring in money. At other times, I have worked with my hands, doing all sorts of jobs, in order to pay my bills and continue to minister. I have seen my salary rise, and I have seen it fall. In no case did I think my ministry was over at a place because I had to take a cut in pay.

An old practice in Baptist churches by unsaved church members and leaders has been to withhold tithes and offerings when they wanted the preacher to leave. This is called "starving out" the minister. I don't think that a church should be able to starve out a preacher. What I mean by that is, if the offerings go down, and he believes that God wants him to continue pastoring those people, he should get a job like Paul did, work with his hands, and keep on in the work of the ministry until God provides otherwise.

I say that YOU CANNOT HIRE GOD'S MAN. You can call him, and you can support him financially, but you cannot hire him. If you can hire him, he is not God's man. He is a HIRELING. Listen, beloved, you're dealing with one preacher here who is NOT FOR SALE and NOT FOR HIRE. A fellow came to one of the men in my church and said, "You know, your pastor does a lot of talking against the Southern Baptist Convention. If he had the opportunity to get a big Southern Baptist church, though, and get a big check, he would take that SBC church in a minute." That man was a LIAR. I won't consider leaving my church for another FUNDAMENTAL church over an increase in salary, let alone a church that is supporting the corrupt, apostate Cooperative Program of the Southern Baptist Convention. I left the SBC in 1972. I don't preach in Southern Baptist churches. I don't visit their revival meetings. I'm not about to consider being a pastoral candidate for one of their churches.

THEY WANT THE WOMEN.

> **2 Timothy 3:6   For of this sort are they which creep into houses, and lead captive silly women laden with sins, led away with divers lusts,**

I remember an interview with a popular minister, one of the devil's imitation shepherds, that was printed in a local newspaper. He was one of these "health, wealth, and prosperity preachers." He was a lady's man, and the interviewer asked him about his women. He was married, but he made no bones about the fact that he had sexual relations outside of wedlock. He said something to the effect that, "If you are asking me how many women I have, I'm not going to tell you that."

Listen; if a man won't tell you how many women he has, he has too many. I have no problem telling you how many women I have. I have ONE. I am still married to my first wife. God willing, she will be my last. I jokingly say that I married her when we were both too young to know any better, in 1971. After nearly 50 years, I don't know any better today than to just stay married to her, "until death us do part." Outside of my conversion to Christ, getting married to my wife was the best thing that happened to me in my entire life.

Jimmy Swaggart taught false doctrine in his crusades in the evenings, and after the services he went to hotels with whores. He did this repeatedly. It looked like he was going to get away with it until he made a fellow minister mad by accusing him of wrongdoing. Bad mistake. The man followed Swaggart and caught him on videotape with a "strange woman."

Jim Bakker taught his people how God wanted them to prosper. He and his wife lived lives of luxury. But he got caught with his pants down, too.

Not only do the devil's shepherds want the wealth and the women, but also ...

THEY WANT THE WEAK. The Bible says these hirelings beguile "unstable souls" (2 Pet. 2:14). They prey on new converts and on people who have never gotten grounded in the faith. We have had people get saved in this church and get hoodwinked by the devil before they ever got grounded. We had others join this church who weren't grounded when they came here, and they messed up before they got established in the word under our ministry. The devil sees these people as easy targets. God's people should be on the lookout for the devil's attempts to get our new and weak brethren.

Finally, I want you to ...

CONSIDER THE ABILITY OF THE DEVIL'S IMITATION SHEPHERDS

I suppose this section of the chapter should actually be titled, "Consider the INABILITY" rather than the ABILITY "of the Devil's Imitation Shepherds." The devil has a lot of power, under God's permissive will, as will be pointed out in Chapter 8 on "Imitation Signs and Wonders." However, his ministers are handicapped. There are some things that they just simply don't do well. This inability is described in the book of Isaiah:

> **Isaiah 56:10-11 His watchmen are blind: they are all ignorant, they are all dumb dogs, they cannot bark; sleeping, lying down, loving to slumber. 11 Yea, they are greedy dogs which can never have enough, and they are shepherds that cannot understand: they all look to their own way, every one for his gain, from his quarter.**

Ministers are supposed to be watchmen. A good pastor is concerned about the spiritual welfare of his parishioners. He doesn't want the devil to overtake them. He watches for the souls of his flock. The Bible says,

> **Hebrews 13:17 Obey them that have the rule over you, and submit yourselves: for they watch for your souls, as they that must give account, that they may do it with joy, and not with grief: for that is unprofitable for you.**

THEY HAVE NO ABILITY TO PERCEIVE THE TRUTH. According to Isa. 56:10, the devil's imitation shepherds are "blind: they are all ignorant." Verse 11 says that "... they are shepherds that cannot understand." Yes, they are blind indeed. They are blinded by the god of this world.

> **2 Corinthians 4:3-4 But if our gospel be hid, it is hid to them that are lost: 4 In whom the god of this world hath blinded the minds of them which believe not, lest the light of the glorious gospel of Christ, who is the image of God, should shine unto them.**

They are unregenerated, so they do not have the Spirit of God, who gives people the ability to understand God's truth.

> **1 Corinthians 2:14 But the natural man receiveth not the things of the Spirit of God: for they are foolishness unto him: neither can he know them, because they are spiritually discerned.**

These imitation shepherds are blind leaders of the blind. A man can spend hours and hours studying under the devil's counterfeit preachers, and he will get absolutely NO TRUTH from the Lord as a result. As a matter of fact, when a person sits under the teaching of these false shepherds, he is headed for destruction.

> **Matthew 15:14 Let them alone: they be blind leaders of the blind. And if the blind lead the blind, both shall fall into the ditch.**

Paul described them this way:

> **1 Timothy 1:6 From which some having swerved have turned aside unto vain jangling; 7 Desiring to be teachers of the law; understanding neither what they say, nor whereof they affirm.**

I love the way that's worded. The teaching of the devil's imitation shepherds is nothing more than "vain jangling." It's just so much noise. They have no understanding of what the scriptures SAY, nor of what they TEACH.

THEY HAVE NO ABILITY TO PREACH THE TRUTH. Further, Isa. 56:10 says of the devil's shepherds that "they are all dumb dogs, they cannot bark." Everyone of these counterfeit shepherds has a degree, the D.D. degree -- Dumb Dogs. The preacher in this passage is compared to a watchdog that is guarding the flock from the wolf and the lion. God counts on the shepherd dog to bark when danger nears. The comparison is to preaching.

What good is a watchdog if he can't bark? False prophets don't warn God's people about heretical teaching, because the false prophets are DOING the heretical teaching! If they call something heresy, you can just about always bank on the fact that the heresy is BIBLE TRUTH. For instance, when someone says that a person who believes his Bible is the word of God is a member of the "King James Cult," you can safely assume that what he calls heresy is absolute truth. If you find one of these ministers of the devil saying that the doctrine of eternal security is a damnable heresy, then you can mark it down: eternal security is PURE doctrine from the word of God.

The devil's ministers, using "good words and fair speeches," don't do much real preaching. They make people feel GOOD. This is a characteristic of the last days.

> **2 Timothy 4:3-4 For the time will come when they will not endure sound doctrine; but after their own lusts shall they heap to themselves teachers, having itching ears; 4 And they shall turn away their ears from the truth, and shall be turned unto fables.**

A phony preacher will be an ear-scratching preacher. He will do whatever makes his congregation feel good. When they turn from one direction to another, he adapts, and he just keeps on scratching. A real preacher's preaching should sometimes OFFEND. A watchdog will bark, and it's not the most pleasing sound in the world. In another place, the preacher's alarm is compared to the sound of a trumpet:

> **Isaiah 58:1 Cry aloud, spare not, lift up thy voice like a trumpet, and shew my people their transgression, and the house of Jacob their sins.**

Have you ever lived with someone who played the trumpet? Occasionally, I will see someone jerk in the auditorium when I suddenly raise my voice in a shout. I have seen a child or two even cup their hands over their ears when I have hollered. That's okay. I would rather run someone off by sounding like a trumpet than keeping them in by scratching their "itching ears."

THEY HAVE NO ABILITY TO PRACTICE THE TRUTH. The devil's watchmen are characterized as "sleeping, lying down, loving to slumber" (Isa. 56:10. They are said to be "greedy dogs which can never have enough," and they look "every one for his gain, from his quarter."

One of the qualifications for a pastor (bishop) is that he not be greedy of filthy lucre (1 Tim. 3:3). On this point, all of the devil's shepherds fall short, because they are ALL greedy dogs, ALL looking to their own way, EVERY ONE for his gain, from his quarter.

For this reason, when the devil's imitation shepherds are examined closely, it will be discovered that they are actually pretty wicked in their private lives. They may put on an outward show, but they have no inward strength to do God's will. The Bible says describes them as

2 Timothy 3:5 Having a form of godliness, but denying the power thereof: from such turn away.

Hopefully you will now be able to recognize the difference between God's true shepherds and the devil's IMITATION SHEPHERDS. The devil is a great counterfeiter, but he, being wicked and less powerful than the Lord, is not able to produce a perfect copy. Observe and take heed.

CHAPTER 7

IMITATION SONGS

Job 38:1-7 Then the LORD answered Job out of the whirlwind, and said, 2 Who is this that darkeneth counsel by words without knowledge? 3 Gird up now thy loins like a man; for I will demand of thee, and answer thou me. 4 Where wast thou when I laid the foundations of the earth? declare, if thou hast understanding. 5 Who hath laid the measures thereof, if thou knowest? or who hath stretched the line upon it? 6 Whereupon are the foundations thereof fastened? or who laid the corner stone thereof; 7 When the morning stars sang together, and all the sons of God shouted for joy?

In studying the great desire of Satan to be "like the most High" (Isa. 14:14) and counterfeit the things of God, we come now to the area of MUSIC. I have pointed out to you a number of things of God that the devil has imitated. In this chapter, I want you to see that the devil counterfeited the Lord's music. His music is in many ways like Christian music. I will point out the differences, and I'm going to show that he has tried to corrupt Christian music by mixing HIS music with GOD'S music. The devil's music is RELIGIOUS music. That is, it affects the heart. It has to do with one's devotions, his passions, and his purity. Satan's music affects the family. Satan's music affects the church!

Music is the universal language. People from all kinds of languages and cultures can listen to the same music and appreciate it. One of the things that I believe softened the hearts of many people in Soviet Russia toward the idea of trying to get along with the United States toward the end of "the Cold War" was the fact that they enjoyed our BAD MUSIC. That's right! I know that President Reagan's push for a strong U.S. military was a great incentive. I know their own political, social, and economic problems in the U.S.S.R. were involved. But there was more to it than that. If I'm not mistaken, Michael Jackson performed in Russia and was loved by their young people. Bruce Springsteen sang to the Russians and was received with open arms. How could the Russians even think of blowing up the country where these two music idols lived?

Music is a universal language. It speaks to the heart. It speaks to the spirit. Even if no one knows exactly what is being sung, there is a message being conveyed by the music. Because of that, it behooves us to be very, very careful about music. Music speaks, and it has an effect on the inside of the hearer. Some people believe that music even has an effect on their plants. That's right. There are some people who are very particular about this; of course, these are the same people who TALK to their plants. Some people that believe music has an effect on their animals, and some of them will even play a particular type of music at night to put their pets to sleep.

I certainly do believe that music has an effect on animals. Not only do I believe music is a universal language but that it is a spiritual force that has been around long before the world was ever created. When God pressured Job about things he didn't know, He named off some things that were beyond Job's knowledge. He said, "Job, ol' boy, where were you when I laid the foundations of the earth?" (That's the ORV, the O'Neal Revised Version.) God said that when the world was created, "the morning stars sang together, and all the sons of God shouted for joy" (Job 38:7). These stars, beloved, are no doubt a reference to angels, as they are called in Rev. 1:20. There was music going on when the world was created. "In the beginning God created the heaven and the earth," and when the Lord spoke them into existence, the angels of God were singing. Perhaps they were singing something like, "This is My Father's World."

So, music has been around for a long time. Heavenly creatures utilized music when the world was created. I believe that spiritual beings use music today. Among those spiritual beings is ... THE DEVIL. Therefore, we come to this chapter, "IMITATION SONGS." First, of all, consider with me:

THE POLLUTION OF SATAN'S IMITATION SONGS

I believe there was a time when Lucifer was associated with music that was right, holy, and good. Some people have said that the devil, before he fell, was the choir leader of heaven. I don't know if that is so, but the Bible describes him in Ezek. 28, and says,

> **Ezekiel 28:13 Thou hast been in Eden the garden of God; every precious stone was thy covering, the sardius, topaz, and**

the diamond, the beryl, the onyx, and the jasper, the sapphire, the emerald, and the carbuncle, and gold: the workmanship of thy tabrets and of thy pipes was prepared in thee in the day that thou wast created.

IT WAS HEAVENLY AT ONE TIME. We're going to come back to that business about the tabrets and pipes, but I want to say that before iniquity was found in him (Ezek. 28:15), the music of Lucifer was HEAVENLY. There was a time when he was called "the anointed cherub that covereth" (Ezek. 28:14). You might remember that in the construction of the tabernacle there were cherubim who covered the ark of the tabernacle with their wings. There are cherubim around the throne of God in heaven. Four of them are described in Rev. 4, but there were probably FIVE originally, one of them being Lucifer. At that time he had tabrets and pipes in him, perhaps as part of his being. There was music in heaven, and Lucifer was in the middle of it.

By the way, heaven is a musical place. Did you know they sing in heaven? Those of you who don't sing God's praises down here aren't very heavenly. If you claim to be saved, but you don't sing, you need to get right with God. There is singing in heaven! I suggest that you learn the tunes now, so you won't be so stupid-looking up there! Isn't it embarrassing to get in a church service and you can't participate in the singing because you don't know the words nor the music? That's a very uncomfortable feeling. I have had it happen to me several times over the years when I have visited churches who spontaneously sang choruses that the church family knew but that I had never heard.

It was heavenly music, and I can imagine what it must have been like. I don't think that it was much like what you hear on most "Christian" radio stations today. There is not much on Christian radio, by the way, that should be listened to by a Bible-believer. I don't recommend you spend much time at all listening to the average Christian radio station.

IT WAS HOLY AT ONE TIME. The first music was HOLY music. Its themes were not drinking, fornication, and rebellion. It was composed to praise the name of the Lord! When you listened to the first music, you didn't think about going out and rebelling against the establishment; you didn't dream of committing adultery; it motivated you to serve God!

IT WAS HAPPY AT ONE TIME. I believe that music was HAPPY music. I don't think that the music of heaven is usually done in a minor key. The Bible says:

> **Psalms 100:1-2 Make a joyful noise unto the LORD, all ye lands. 2 Serve the LORD with gladness: come before his presence with singing.**

You know, there may be some energy in the music of this world, but a great deal of the world's music is full of anger, bitterness, and/or sorrow. A whole branch of music is called the "blues," a sad, gloomy style that originated with Africans and made its way into the New Orleans night clubs. God's music, on the other hand, is HAPPY music!

IT WAS HEALTHY AT ONE TIME. I also believe that the first music was HEALTHY music. That's right. I agree with the idea that music has an effect on your physical, mental, emotional, and spiritual well being. Music can soothe, and it can irritate. It can arouse, and it can sedate. I believe that music can make your blood pressure go up or down. Music can help encourage small children to run to and fro. If you don't believe that it can affect a child's body, put a toddler in front of a TV set that's playing rock music. Before you know it, that child will be dancing! -- and it won't be a HOLY dance!! You don't have to take a child to dancing classes to get it to dance; MUSIC will teach the child to dance.

But Satan fell. Satan was polluted. When Satan got kicked out of his position, he began to produce fallen, sinful, rebellious music. Let's observe, after the fall of Lucifer,

THE PATTERN OF SATAN'S IMITATION SONGS

In Ezekiel, two particular instruments of music were mentioned: the tabrets and the pipes of Lucifer. Those terms have to do with modern drums and organs, as well as other wind instruments. Earlier I made reference to the "blues." Beloved, that "jazz" music once identified with the French Quarter of New Orleans, which evolved from the Negro folk music known as the blues, was SATANIC. That music had its origin in AFRICA.

The Bible has a good bit to say about Africa, although the most interesting facts are about Northern Africa, particularly Egypt. When the children of Israel escaped out of the bondage of Egypt, a "mixed multitude" went up with them (Ex. 12:38). That is, some Jews had married Africans and had half-breeds in the congregation of Israel. This "mixt multitude," as the spelling has it in Num. 11:4, later led the children of Israel into angering God (Num. 11:10) by their constant griping about the quality of food they were getting. Sound familiar?

With that in mind, think about what happened when God gave Moses the ten commandments for His people. Moses spent 40 days and nights with God in the mountain, while the children of Israel waited. Instead of having prayer meetings, however, the Israelites got involved in idolatry, dancing, and nakedness. When Moses went down from his "mountain-top" experience with the Lord (my, that must have been some kind of an experience!) he was greeted by some unusual sounds.

> **Exodus 32:15-18 And Moses turned, and went down from the mount, and the two tables of the testimony were in his hand: the tables were written on both their sides; on the one side and on the other were they written. 16 And the tables were the work of God, and the writing was the writing of God, graven upon the tables. 17 And when Joshua heard the noise of the people as they shouted, he said unto Moses, There is a noise of war in the camp. 18 And he said, It is not the voice of them that shout for mastery, neither is it the voice of them that cry for being overcome: but the noise of them that sing do I hear.**

What a significant time in history! God took an individual into a mountain alone, and spoke to Him one on one, giving him infallible guidelines for human conduct. With His own finger, God wrote on tables of stone what He wanted man to do. While such a spiritual experience was going on with God and His man, the people of God were forgetful, backslidden, carnal, and wicked. This is typical of the fact that many times God's preacher spends time with God getting God's message to bring to the people on Sunday. When it is time to deliver the message, however, the people of God are so far out of touch with God and are so worldly that they can't appreciate the wonderful tidings from heaven!

Joshua thought that he heard the sounds of war in the camp. He concluded that some enemy had attacked the camp while they were in the mount. No doubt he was alarmed and was ready to enter the fray and give his life, if need be, to defend his brethren. Isn't something suspicious when you hear music of "worship" (the children of Israel were in an idolatrous worship service) and mistake the music for the sounds of war? There ought to be a difference between a worship service's music and the sounds of a battlefield!

Joshua kept listening.

> **Exodus 32:18 And he said, It is not the voice of them that shout for mastery, neither is it the voice of them that cry for being overcome: but the noise of them that sing do I hear.**

Let me mention a few things to you about the PATTERN of the devil's imitation songs. He has fooled many people into accepting HIS music as being that of the LORD, but there are distinctive differences. When I talk about the pattern of Satan's music, I'm not talking about what is sensationalized in books and digital recordings about subliminal messages, backward masking, and such. The devil has managed to sneak his music in without having to play it backwards, my friend.

Often Contemporary Christian Music (CCM) is written so that the words refer to the Lord in very generic terms. One piece of music that was popular in youth choirs in the 60's and 70's spoke of the Lord as "He" throughout the song, without ever mentioning who He IS! The name of Jesus, much less the full title of the Lord Jesus Christ, never occurred in the song a single time. This is significant, because it is by the name of JESUS that we are saved.

> **Acts 4:12 Neither is there salvation in any other: for there is none other name under heaven given among men, whereby we must be saved.**

However, the devil's music is identified not so much by its lyrics as it is by its BEAT. I don't think Joshua heard the lyrics of that African orgy that disguised itself as a call to worship. I think he heard what you hear when a young person drives by your house with a stereo system in his car that cost more than the automobile itself. You know what I'm talking about. You've seen your silverware jump up and down on the table when one of these powerful bass speakers does its thing near your place.

SATAN'S MUSIC HAS AN ANAPESTIC BEAT. This is a technical term, but it describes the beat of the devil's imitation songs, "like that of the most High." Most Christian music is of two variations. It's either a variation of 4/4 time or 3/4 time. I like to think of them as War and Worship time or March and Meditation time. These songs in your songbook will either be peppy songs of praise and service, written in 4/4 time or a variation thereof, or they are more devotional songs, written in 3/4 time or a variation of it. The anapestic beat is actually a corruption of 4/4 time. Instead of being four beats of equal length with an accent on the first and third beats, it is composed of two short, unaccented beats followed by a longer, accented beat. Unfortunately, I cannot reproduce this for your ear in a book, but if you will listen carefully to almost any song you hear that has been written in the last 50 years, you will be able to hear that beat in the background. It's behind all rock music, all country music, and it is behind 99% of all Christian music written in the last half of the century.

SATAN'S MUSIC HAS AN AFRICAN (EGYPTIAN) BEAT. This beat is a JUNGLE beat. One-Two THREE, One-Two THREE, One-Two THREE. The music the Israelites were involved in was music that they had carried with them out of Africa, the land of Ham, specifically the land of Egypt. Anyone who knows his Bible knows that Egypt is a "type" (picture) of the world, and that it is one of the worst places with which anyone should be associated. By the way, I didn't mention it in Chapter 5 on "Imitation Scriptures," but the new versions of the Bible are from a textual line that is labeled an "Egyptian" type of text. That's right! Those Bibles are associated with Egypt, especially the city of Alexandria, in the continent of Africa.

God brought His people AWAY from the evil influence of Egypt. When they departed, however, the Bible says that they took a "mixed multitude" with them. These were half-breeds, the result of intermarriage between the Jewish people and the African people. That's where the Jews picked up some of their false worship, some of their immorality, and some of their music. It's African music. There is something peculiar about Africa in its relationship to God. The Lord warned against going down to Egypt, and against leaning upon Egypt for support.

SATAN'S MUSIC HAS AN ANTAGONISTIC (WARLIKE) BEAT. As I just mentioned, the beat is straight out of the jungle. When someone drives by your house and their car stereo system is playing modern music, about all you can hear is that antagonistic beat. When Joshua heard it, he just KNEW the children of Israel were under attack. He fully expected to arrive on the scene of a full-scale war. This beat stirs people to fight, to rebel, and secondarily, to dance, especially in a sensuous fashion or in preparation for immorality.

SATAN'S MUSIC HAS AN ANIMALISTIC BEAT. The children of Israel were behaving like animals. They stripped their clothes off, they were dancing around, and had no sense of God about them at all. You can't get away from the fact that this beat is jungle-oriented. It is no coincidence that as rock music gained in popularity, the bands who played it went by such names as the Monkeys, the Animals, and Three Dog Night.

THE POPULARITY OF SATAN'S IMITATION SONGS

The devil's music is fallen music. It is the music of the WORLD, as well as of the flesh, and of the devil. Therefore, the world loves it. Given enough time, even the older generation will enjoy the newer music, because it all has the same beat.

When this music is incorporated into church services, it attracts the world. If the music were not WRONG, EVIL, and SINFUL, that would not necessarily be a bad thing. The fact that it appeals to the world, however, should make a discerning Christian immediately suspicious, especially considering what the Lord and Savior Jesus Christ said in:

> **Luke 16:15 And he said unto them, Ye are they which justify yourselves before men; but God knoweth your hearts: for that which is highly esteemed among men is abomination in the sight of God.**

In other words, if the world likes it, you can just about always be assured that it is 100% WRONG. If the world likes it, God hates it, and vice-versa.

I'm going to break the devil's music into three groups:

There is the **HONKY-TONK CROWD MUSIC.** You can drive by some churches at night and you can't really tell the difference between their music and that found in your country western nightclub. They have the same instruments played exactly the same way. All of this music (not necessarily the lyrics) is associated with adultery, fornication, rebellion, and other undesirable traits. Country western musicians sometimes act like their music is so much better than that wicked, wild, rock music. There's not really that much difference. Both types of music promote wrongdoing. The country western music is the same in nature as rock music; it just runs about 20 years behind it in debauchery.

In the 1960's and early 1970's, country western musicians looked like human beings, and the rock musicians looked like bearded women who hadn't bathed in six months. Now nearly all of the musicians look the same. Not too long ago I saw a country western musician I had not seen on television since my youth. I was shocked. He looked awful.

It is a shame that many fundamental churches have gotten hooked on this honky-tonk music. They still sing hymns from the hymn book, but 90% of their "special" music is country western. They call it Southern Gospel, but it is nothing more than the Grand Ole Opry with Christian lyrics.

There is the **HIPPY-ROCK CROWD MUSIC**. Rock music is built around two main themes: sex and rebellion. For most rock musicians, love equals sex, and sex equals love. The rock style music permeates all of the liberal churches. Nearly all special music in the Southern Baptist churches is rock, and fundamental churches are not too far behind the Southern Baptists.

There is the **HEAVENLY CROWD MUSIC**. Unfortunately, nearly every church musician is someone who listens to straight secular country western or rock music, or he listens to a variation of them with Christian lyrics. Believers who listen to "Christian" music on Christian television and radio stations are not going to be able to perform the right music at church. They have been polluted. We need a revival in our churches about our music! If you're a fundamentalist, you might be interested in my little book, "How Bad Music is Killing Our Fundamental Churches."

THE PRODUCT OF SATAN'S IMITATION SONGS

Music has an effect. The devil knows that. That's why he has infiltrated God's people, their homes, and their habits with his music in every way possible. You can't get away from it. It's in the grocery stores, in the malls, and in the churches. You shop by it, you work by it, and you worship by it.

In the days of the prophet Daniel, there was a decree that came forth from the king, in which all the subjects of the kingdom were commanded to worship a golden image that he had constructed.

Daniel 3:4-5 Then an herald cried aloud, To you it is commanded, O people, nations, and languages, 5 That at what time ye hear the sound of the cornet, flute, harp, sackbut, psaltery, dulcimer, and all kinds of musick, ye fall down and worship the golden image that Nebuchadnezzar the king hath set up:

What does Satan's music produce? It produces several things, and none of them are good. I'll take just a little space here to mention a few of them.

SATAN'S IMITATION SONGS PRODUCE DRUG USE. Drugs and professional musicians always go together. That's because the musicians perform Satan's music. Before rock music, it was common for jazz musicians to be drug addicts.

SATAN'S IMITATION SONGS PRODUCE DANCING. I'm not talking about any kind of holy dance, either. The dancing produced by Satan's music is a sexual, jungle dance.

SATAN'S IMITATION SONGS PRODUCE DEFILEMENT. The African jungle beat of Satan's music is a SEX beat. The tempo doesn't always have to be fast to have the desired effect. Slow music can still have the African beat and be sensual in nature.

SATAN'S IMITATION SONGS PRODUCE DEVIL POSSESSION. Music doesn't just affect the physical world; it has an effect on the spiritual world.

> **1 Samuel 16:23 And it came to pass, when the evil spirit from God was upon Saul, that David took an harp, and played with his hand: so Saul was refreshed, and was well, and the evil spirit departed from him.**

There is no mention in the above verse of lyrics, just a musical instrument. Apparently, then, GOOD music REPELS unclean spirits. It follows that BAD music must ATTRACT them.

Music is a powerful force. It behooves us to recognize that Satan has music "like that of the most high." It's close, but it's COUNTERFEIT. The words may resemble the music of the saints of God, but we must be careful. Sometimes the lyrics just use the words "He" or "You" and leave out the words "God" or "Jesus." Additionally, if the music is bad, there will be a bad effect, even if the lyrics are acceptable.

If you have SATAN'S music in your house, get rid of it. If you have his music in your heart, get rid of it. Replace it with God's music. Don't let your spirit be corrupted by IMITATION SONGS.

CHAPTER 8

IMITATION SIGNS AND WONDERS

Deuteronomy 13:1-5 If there arise among you a prophet, or a dreamer of dreams, and giveth thee a sign or a wonder, 2 And the sign or the wonder come to pass, whereof he spake unto thee, saying, Let us go after other gods, which thou hast not known, and let us serve them; 3 Thou shalt not hearken unto the words of that prophet, or that dreamer of dreams: for the LORD your God proveth you, to know whether ye love the LORD your God with all your heart and with all your soul. 4 Ye shall walk after the LORD your God, and fear him, and keep his commandments, and obey his voice, and ye shall serve him, and cleave unto him. 5 And that prophet, or that dreamer of dreams, shall be put to death; because he hath spoken to turn you away from the LORD your God, which brought you out of the land of Egypt, and redeemed you out of the house of bondage, to thrust thee out of the way which the LORD thy God commanded thee to walk in. So shalt thou put the evil away from the midst of thee.

In the above passage the Lord told His people to not pay attention to anyone who is a false teacher, even if he has signs or wonders that come to pass! Rather, the Lord told them to "obey HIS voice." The Lord has given us a Bible, His word, and He wants us to live by it.

Jesus said that in the great temptation in:

Luke 4:4 And Jesus answered him, saying, It is written, That man shall not live by bread alone, but by every word of God.

Yes, you're supposed to live by "every word of God." Of course, if you are reading one of the newer "perversions" of scripture, such as the New World Translation of the Jehovah's False Witnesses, you won't know that, because Luke 4:4 in the NWT leaves out the words "but by every word of God." You also won't know that if you are reading Luke 4:4 from the TEV (Today's English Version, also known as the Good News Bible), the

New American Standard Bible, or the Living Bible. As a matter of fact, even the NIV (New International Version) omits the last words of the verse. Do you realize that in many places where the King James Bible gets corrupted in the new versions, there is no real difference between the New International Version and the JFW (Jehovah's False Witnesses) New World Translation? I pointed these things out in chapter 5 on Imitation Scriptures.

In this book I have tried to show you that the devil's great desire is to "be like the most High" (Isa. 14:12-14). He imitates God. He is the greatest deceiver of all time. He counterfeits the things of God. In this final chapter I want to point out that the devil has IMITATION SIGNS AND WONDERS. That is what Deut. 13:1-5 is about.

Of course I understand that most of what is done by professed miracle workers is just sleight-of-hand trickery. I am amazed that so many folks are deceived by that which is OBVIOUSLY fake. Some people don't seem to understand the difference between reality and make-believe. I suppose that the same people who think "championship rasslin'" is really a competitive sport also think Benny Hinn's healing line is an exhibition of God knocking people backward by His Holy Spirit. It is actually difficult for me to comprehend that some people can't tell the difference between such ENTERTAINMENT and the real thing. I guess that I can express how I usually feel about such spiritual ignorance by saying: Just when you think something is idiot-proof, they make a better idiot.

I don't understand how any discerning Christian could be fooled by a fraud like Oral Roberts, Benny Hinn, or any of the rest of them. A friend of mine pastored in Orlando where Hinn's headquarters was located. My pastor friend happened to see Hinn's healing line on television one day, and, lo and behold, there was one of his men, a member of the church's deaf ministry, standing in the healing line. Hinn breathed on him, knocking him over (some of the young men in my church can also do that trick), after which he proclaimed him to be healed. On the next Sunday, however, the man was back in his usual church, in the deaf ministry, unable to hear.

About 99.99 percent of this business is phony. I never worry for one moment that I am "blaspheming the Holy Spirit" when I point this out. I haven't committed that sin, and none of your acquaintances have done so, either. No one whom you know, since Calvary, has blasphemed the Holy Ghost, as the sin is defined in scripture (see Mark 3:28-30 where the sin is to say that JESUS had an unclean spirit while He walked the earth). I've spoken nose-to-nose and face-to-face with a lot of these people, and I say with utmost confidence that nearly ALL of what has been proclaimed to be signs and wonders has been found, upon examination, to be a sham.

I was talking to a charismaniac many years ago who asked me if I had heard about a bunch of Baptists out in Texas who had received the Holy Spirit (interpretation: they were deceived by an unclean spirit and embraced the charismatic movement). I said, "Barry, there is a great deal of difference between receiving the Holy Spirit and speaking in a bunch of gibberish."

"You just don't believe what the Bible says about the gift of tongues," he replied.

"Certainly I do," I said, "but those Baptists didn't get the gift of tongues, and neither did you."

"Oh, yes," he affirmed, "I speak in tongues."

"Good. Say something!"

Shaken, he protested, "The Holy Ghost doesn't work that way."

"Sure he does," I answered. "The Bible says that the spirits of the prophets are subject to the prophets. If you have the gift, USE it. Let's see it."

He was speechless. I prodded: "Look. If I could show you that your church contradicts the Bible, would you forsake your church and adhere to the Bible?"

Enraged, he began turning purple, and he spouted, "MY church won't contradict the Bible; MY church IS the Bible!" I'm not fooling you. That's exactly what he said.

That man didn't have the gift of tongues. He had been lying through his teeth. The truth is, if he was a missionary preparing to go to the foreign field, he would have had to enter language school, just like ALL charismatic missionaries do. Have you ever wondered why charismatic missionaries go to language school when they claim that God has given them the gift of tongues (languages)? He was caught red-handed. Otherwise, he would not have said something so stupid.

I looked the fellow in the eye and said, "The truth of the matter is, bud, NOT that God does not work that way, but rather that you don't have the gift of tongues, you have NEVER had the gift of tongues, and you KNOW it. YOU are a FAKE!"

Having said all of this about phonies and fakes, I want to say that the devil CAN supply signs and wonders like those of the most High. The devil CAN work miracles. He can empower his children to work miracles. If God allows him to do it, the devil could take an unsaved person and give him the ability to speak in a language he has never studied. You see, the devil is in the business of IMITATING the signs and wonders of the most High. Those of you who have read your Bibles ought to know that.

I want to say, first of all, that:

SATAN CAN PROVIDE SUPERNATURAL MIRACLES

I'm not talking about any of those hoaxes now. I'm talking about supernatural stuff. By the way, don't think that I'm prejudiced against the charismatic movement. I have checked it out firsthand. I have been to the meetings. I've sat under the tents. I have heard the men preach. I have heard the women preach. I've had their preachers try to cast devils out of me and my buddies, to prophesy about me, and to prove themselves to me. I have not been impressed by any of it.

Having said all of that, I believe the devil is able to deceive people by means of supernatural miracles. The Bible says,

> **Deuteronomy 13:1-2a If there arise among you a prophet, or a dreamer of dreams, and giveth thee a sign or a wonder, 2 And the sign or the wonder come to pass ...**

That is, it is possible that a false prophet might give you a sign or a wonder that actually takes place, and there's absolutely nothing pretended at all. It is a supernatural wonder!

Some of you people wouldn't know what to say if you were with a Catholic person in front of a statue of Mary, and the statue began to cry. You know the Catholics have had a tradition of miracles, signs, and wonders long before Amie Semple McPherson got herself filled with unclean spirits around the first of this century. The Catholics have had visions, signs, and wonders, drawing people from all across the world. If you, as a Bible-believing Christian, were standing in front of a statue of Mary that started crying, and your Catholic friend said to you, "See, that shows you for certain that the Catholic faith is God's way," what would you say?

I'll tell you what I would say. I would say, "Do you want to know why she is crying? It's due to the fact that she knows that bowing down before her statue is idolatry!" Amen! You and I should judge everything by the word of God, not by something that amazes our senses! If God allows a statue of Mary to cry, I have a strong idea of why He allows it to happen. It's because He's ASHAMED of the Catholics who worship Mary as the Queen of Heaven. Mary is not the Queen of Heaven. She doesn't DESIRE to be the Queen of Heaven. She just wants to glorify the Son of God!

The Bible teaches that in the coming time known as the Tribulation period there will be signs and wonders manifesting themselves.

> **Revelation 16:14 For they are the spirits of devils, working miracles, which go forth unto the kings of the earth and of the whole world, to gather them to the battle of that great day of God Almighty.**

Beloved, the Bible says in that verse that spirits of devils can work miracles! Read it! Believe it! People look at these signs, and they believe the message of the sign workers. Listen, my friend, it is not a noble characteristic to believe God on the basis of seeing some sign or a wonder. There is nothing commendable about your attitude expressed when you say, "God did this in my presence, so I KNOW He is real!"

> **Romans 10:17 So then faith cometh by hearing, and hearing by the word of God.**

I know that the Lord is real, because the BOOK says so!

You say, "Preacher, what about these signs? Don't they prove that God is in the charismatic movement?" The Bible says,

> **Matthew 12:39a But he answered and said unto them, An evil and adulterous generation seeketh after a sign...**

If you are looking for some proof of God in a sign or a wonder, that is a sure indication that you are a wicked and adulterous individual. That includes you, your mother, and your sweet old Aunt Mary, who has watched Oral Roberts on television every week for the last 200 years! You are an "evil and adulterous generation"!

You say, "Preacher, you don't seem to have the sweet spirit of Christ." You just wait. I haven't even gotten to a discussion of the cleansing of the temple yet. The rough stuff is still yet to come.

Do you not believe that the devil can do supernatural signs and wonders? Do you remember when God delivered the children of Israel out of Egypt? He used signs and wonders and was magnified in the sight of all of Egypt. If you know your Bible, however, you also know that for every sign and wonder that Moses and Aaron performed, the magicians of Pharaoh, children of Satan, did likewise. Those magicians turned their rods into serpents. That was no sleight-of-hand, friend. That was real! What would you think if some modern charismatic conman were to turn a rod into a snake in front of your eyes? Would you think that is a verification of his message?

Moses cast down his rod (he actually did this through his brother, Aaron), and it became a serpent. The magicians cast down their rods, and, wonder of wonders, they ALSO turned into serpents! That's not all. These magicians were able to turn water into blood! This really happened! This wasn't just a stunt! This wasn't like the "make believe" miracle performed at every "Mass" during the "Eucharist." I'm referring to the deceit performed when gullible people are convinced that the wine and the bread have been transformed miraculously into the blood and body of Christ by the priest's magical pronunciation of "Fe Fi Fo Fum, E Pluribus Unum," even though the elements still look, feel, and taste like wine and bread. That "miracle" is called "transubstantiation." Honest observers call it "lunacy." Bible believers call it "baloney" (that's Hebrew for "bologna").

Nor are we talking about the drunk who was pulled over on the side of the highway by the state trooper. When asked if he was drinking, the fellow said, "Naw, suh, I wudn't drinkin'." The policeman asked, "Then what's in the bottle in the front seat?" He answered, "Dat's WATER in dat bottle." The cop opened the bottle, tested it, and said, "Mister, that's not water in this bottle, that's WINE in the bottle.""Wine?" the drunk gasped. "Lawsee mercy, de Lawd has done DONE it AGAIN!"

No, that's just wishful thinking on the part of the drunk who remembered the miracle performed at the wedding in John 2. In Moses' day, those magicians actually turned the water into blood like Moses and Aaron did. It wasn't wishful thinking. It wasn't a trick. It was real.

Another miracle that the magicians performed was to pull multitudes of frogs out of the water on to the land. The reason God allowed them to have this power was to try people to see whether they would go by the word of God or by the signs.

Isaiah 8:20 To the law and to the testimony: if they speak not according to this word, it is because there is no light in them.

My friends, the "proof of the pudding" is THIS BOOK, not some sign or a wonder. God's word is the infallible standard by which ALL things are to be judged, including the supernatural. If someone speaks according to this WORD, there is light in them, signs or no signs. If they speak not according to this WORD, there is NO LIGHT in them, even if they can turn water into blood. You are to live by every word of God, not by miracles. John the Baptist, according to record, did no miracles, but he certainly preached the truth. I think I'll just be a good Baptist and tell the truth, even if I don't do any miracles. By the way, did you know that Jesus, our Lord, never spoke in tongues?

Besides miracles, I want you to understand that:

SATAN CAN PROVIDE SUPERNATURAL MUSCLE

The devil can do amazing physical things with a person's body. I watched a person who weighed just under 132 pounds put a bar on his shoulders, which, with the weights on the ends, weighed 603 pounds. He put this weight on his shoulders, bent down at his knees until his thighs were parallel with the floor, and then rose up again. I watched him with my own peepers. Do you know that what he did is almost miraculous?

You say, "It's in the mind." Sure, that's involved. You say, "It's all technique." Well, that's a factor, too. So, why don't you get a good positive attitude, learn the proper technique, and see if YOU can squat over 600 pounds at a body weight of 130!

Something was going on. I'm not saying he was full of Satan, but there are some strange things that go on in the world of muscle, especially when you get the spirit world involved.

It could be that not every feat of strength that makes the Guinness Book of World Records or some other record book is 100% physical in its achievement. The spirit world is sometimes involved.

That's what Samson's story involved. Samson didn't get his great strength from pumping iron, although he may have exercised regularly. He obtained his awesome power from God's Spirit. If God came upon him, Samson could do great accomplishments, but if God departed from him, he was as weak as any normal man. There is no indication in the Bible that Samson was a huge, muscular man. He may have been. His strength did not come from his workouts at the local gym, however; it came from GOD.

I believe the devil is able to imitate that power. An illustration of that is found in:

> **Mark 5:1-4 And they came over unto the other side of the sea, into the country of the Gadarenes. 2 And when he was come out of the ship, immediately there met him out of the tombs a man with an unclean spirit, 3 Who had his dwelling among the tombs; and no man could bind him, no, not with chains: 4 Because that he had been often bound with fetters and chains, and the chains had been plucked asunder by him, and the fetters broken in pieces: neither could any man tame him.**

This was SUPERNATURAL strength! It wasn't natural. They bound this man with chains, and he just burst them asunder. He had wild strength -- wild, uncontrollable, untamable strength!

We talk about adrenaline and how that some people in life-threatening situations seem to receive a physical ability to do supernatural feats. Anger can have the same effect. If you don't believe that, ask policemen who answer domestic calls in this town. They will go to a little house and open the door to be greeted by a woman not taller than 5'5" and not heavier than 110 pounds who nearly kills them with a butcher knife. Drugs can have a similar result. Again, ask the men of the local police department.

Just recently I heard about a little, frail fellow who nearly beat the daylights out of a couple of law enforcement officers, because he was so wild and uncontrolled. I'll tell you something else: when a person is under the influence of devils, he may also have the ability to do supernatural feats of strength. Someone says, "That person has gone CRAZY!" Yes, he may have gone crazy, but how do you account for the amount of PHYSICAL POWER he has? I'll tell you how. He's full of the devil, brother.

I've even seen small children, and when I say "small," I'm talking about between the ages of five and 10 years old, who could physically overpower a grown woman twice their size and weight. Say what you will, I think I have seen pre-teens who were "chock full" of devils.

This strength from the world of Satan is **WILD** strength. It is not controlled. It is not productive. It is **WORLDLY** strength. It does not have anything to do with strength of character. A person may possess supernatural physical strength and be one of the most immoral, wicked, ungodly people you have ever met.

And it is **WOEFUL** strength, in the sense that it is very, very sad that somebody would be possessed with such raw, physical power and still be unable to break the chains of sin. He may be able to free himself from chains and still be unable to stay away from a little pack of cigarettes or a little bottle of liquor. No man could bind the devil possessed man of the Gadarenes, no, not with chains. But he was ALREADY bound. He was bound by Satan. It took the LORD to come up to him and say, "Loose him; let him go." Amen! When he was "loosed," the book of Luke says he got his clothes on (he had been running around naked, a sure sign of devil possession), and was found sitting at the feet of Jesus, listening to a Bible study! The Bible says that he was "in his right mind." Hallelujah!

Thirdly, it is also apparent that

SATAN CAN PRODUCE A SUPERNATURAL MENTALITY

Many books have been written about the power of the mind. People claim the ability to do all kinds of things with their minds. Some people claim to have the power of total recall; that is, they can remember anything that they choose to remember from any time in their past -- any name they have heard, any line from a book they have read, etc. Some people claim to be able to have the power to move objects with their minds, an ability known as telekinesis. Some of you have seen performances by these people, 99.99% of which were faked.

Do you know that the devil works through the mind? Much of the battle we have with unseen enemies is within our own minds. When the late evangelist Lester Roloff was in jail, he said the devil almost defeated him there in incarceration. He said the devil just about took his mind. Brother Roloff had a disciplined, sharp, godly mind, but the devil really worked him over.

When I say the devil can produce a supernatural mentality, I'm talking about **SUPERNATURAL COMMUNICATIONS**. Extra-Sensory Perception could be Satanic. Women are often thought of as having a sixth sense, referred to as "woman's intuition." But then, we must remember that the devil worked on Eve before Adam, and the woman is called the "weaker vessel" in the Bible. There are folks who claim to have the power to read minds. Others believe they can project thoughts into someone else's mind.

Concerning these supernatural communications, the Bible says,

> **Ecclesiastes 10:20 Curse not the king, no not in thy thought; and curse not the rich in thy bedchamber: for a bird of the air shall carry the voice, and that which hath wings shall tell the matter.**

No doubt most displays of the ability to read the mind of another person are indeed fraudulent. Tricks can be pulled off using "plants" (people who are seated in an audience who have already agreed to cooperate with the psychic), powerful listening devices, transmitters, and such. However, such supernatural communications are indeed possible, because a bird of the air carries the voice, and that which hath wings tells the matter. Spirits are compared to birds in scripture. The Holy Spirit is likened unto a dove, and unclean spirits are compared to unclean and hateful birds (Rev. 18:2; Lk. 8:5) in the Bible. According to Eph. 2:1-2 all unsaved people have at least one unclean spirit. They can travel from one person to another. You see, the expression, "a little bird told me," is a common reference to an awareness that is unexpected, a knowledge of that which should be secret. The idea came from the Bible: Eccl. 10:20 above.

When I refer to supernatural mentality, I am also referring to a **SUPERNATURAL COMPREHENSION**. What is a child prodigy? If an eight-year-old child is able to read and comprehend a semester of college material in a matter of hours, are we to assume that is natural, or is it SUPERnatural? Folks, excuse my grammar, but "it ain't natural" for a four-year-old to be able to handle trigonometry. You say, "Preacher, you just don't know my four-year-old." I don't HAVE to know your four-year-old; I know YOU. You're not going to produce a four-year-old who has such a mental ability.

People will swear that fortune tellers have had a supernatural comprehension about their past, present, and future. So, what are you and I going to say when some unsaved person tells of the remarkable experience he had with a fortune teller? Are we going to call him a liar? The response of our hearts should be:

Isaiah 8:20 To the law and to the testimony: if they speak not according to this word, it is because there is no light in them.

You ask, "What if someone were to tell you, Preacher, that you were going to have a flat tire on your car on Monday morning, and that it would be a sign to you that the God of Abraham, Isaac, and Jacob was not the true God, but that you need to realize that there are other gods more powerful? What if it were to happen just like the psychic predicted?"

Here's what I would do. I would meditate once again upon Deut. 13:1-5:

> **Deuteronomy 13:1-5 If there arise among you a prophet, or a dreamer of dreams, and giveth thee a sign or a wonder, 2 And the sign or the wonder come to pass, whereof he spake unto thee, saying, Let us go after other gods, which thou hast not known, and let us serve them; 3 Thou shalt not hearken unto the words of that prophet, or that dreamer of dreams: for the LORD your God proveth you, to know whether ye love the LORD your God with all your heart and with all your soul. 4 Ye shall walk after the LORD your God, and fear him, and keep his commandments, and obey his voice, and ye shall serve him, and cleave unto him. 5 And that prophet, or that dreamer of dreams, shall be put to death; because he hath spoken to turn you away from the LORD your God, which brought you out of the land of Egypt, and redeemed you out of the house of bondage, to thrust thee out of the way which the LORD thy God commanded thee to walk in. So shalt thou put the evil away from the midst of thee.**

I would count the psychic as being a devil-possessed fortune teller, and instead of taking heed to Satan's servant, I would continue to guide my life by the word of God! What would YOU do?

With regard to a Satanic supernatural mentality, in addition to supernatural communications and a supernatural comprehension, and I am also convinced there are **SUPERNATURAL CHANGES** which can be produced by a mind empowered by Satan. I'm talking about telekinesis, which I mentioned earlier. I'm referring to the ability to bend eating utensils, lift tables, and move objects on a wall by power of the mind.

Finally, I want to say to you that in regard to signs and wonders,

SATAN CAN PRODUCE SUPERNATURAL MUSIC

Years ago someone from a Christian radio station gave me an audio cassette tape that they had received and rejected. So they gave it to me.

I'm not sure why people want to dump their heretical books and materials on me, but it happens from time to time. I haven't listened to the tape in 30 years, and I don't remember exactly its subject matter. I do remember, however, a positively EERIE female voice and some definitely "spooky" background music on the tape. I was so impressed (not in a favorable way, mind you), that I wanted to see if it affected other believers like it did me. I had never heard anything like it. I probably shouldn't have done this, but I took a few of our Christian school workers, one at a time, and shut them up in a room, with the lights out, to listen to the tape. I only allowed them to listen to a couple of minutes of the tape, but that was plenty. Each one of them exited the room with the same impression: THE MATERIAL ON THE TAPE WAS DEVILISH.

By the way, my school staff members have never been the same. The teachers with the glazed look in their eyes are those who listened to that tape around 30 years ago. Some of you did not know our teachers before that experience; they were actually in their right minds back in those days. (I'm teasing!)

I believe the Devil is in the music business. I don't want to rehash everything that we covered in chapter 7, but don't forget what the Bible said about Satan:

> **Ezekiel 28:13-14 Thou hast been in Eden the garden of God; every precious stone was thy covering, the sardius, topaz, and the diamond, the beryl, the onyx, and the jasper, the sapphire, the emerald, and the carbuncle, and gold: the workmanship of thy tabrets and of thy pipes was prepared in thee in the day that thou wast created. 14 Thou art the anointed cherub that covereth; and I have set thee so: thou wast upon the holy mountain of God; thou hast walked up and down in the midst of the stones of fire.**

Someone has said that the Devil was the choir leader of heaven. I don't know if that is true, but I do believe he was associated with music. Tabrets and pipes were prepared in him when he was created (Ezek. 28:13). When he fell from heaven (Isa. 14:12-14), his music fell with him.

Think of this supernatural work of Satan in regard to **DANCE MUSIC.** I'm sure many of you don't connect dance music with unclean spirits, but you need to study the account of the sin of Israel while Moses was in the mount getting the 10 commandments. The children of Israel began worshiping a golden calf. They took off their clothes, and they began to dance. If you want to know what the dance was like, either visit African jungle tribes, or certain charismatic churches in California. Joshua heard the music as he escorted his mentor, Moses, back to camp, and he mistook the music for the sound of WAR. You know, if you can't tell the difference between two armies fighting, screaming, and hollering, and a choir singing a hymn, you have a real problem somewhere! Joshua had no idea the Israelites were merely dancing to the beat of a "boom box," as they celebrated their "liberty in the spirit." He didn't know they were doing "Christian rap music"; it sounded like a CONFLICT to him!

Those Israelites, descendants of Abraham, Isaac, and Jacob, were having a worship service, but they weren't worshiping God. They were worshiping SATAN. And they had his music to "put them in the spirit."

Some of you fools watch that charismatic stuff on television with all of that Hollywood makeup, movements, music and DANCING, and you think somehow the Lord God is involved in all that. You say, "Don't call me a fool, Preacher." Then don't ACT like one. GROW UP. Get some discernment. Beloved, that dancing is nowhere near the dance David practiced. It is closer to Michael Jackson than it is to King David. Of course, for the country western addicts, they will have a few numbers performed by folks who will sing and dance to the style of the Statler Brothers, Roy Acuff, Kenny Rogers, Porter Wagoner, Buck Owens, and Roy Clark.

The Israelites danced while they worshiped, to Satanic, Egyptian music, that sounded more like WAR than WORSHIP.

The devil provides **DEVOTIONAL MUSIC** as well as DANCE MUSIC. By the way, some of the most immoral people you ever met are those who are involved in this wicked, Hellywood type of Christianity. They put on a good act while they are on stage, but if you knew them personally, you would find them to be just as corrupt in their character as the most carnal Christian you ever ran into.

People the world over loved (and many still do) Jimmy Swaggart. I even knew Baptists who loved his music, because he made them feel good. Brother, it was a feeling, all right, but it wasn't of God. Jimmy crooned, swayed, and tickled the ivory keys on his piano before the thousands who attended his crusades. All the while he was chasing whores at night and taking them into motel rooms. The man was wicked, but gullible religious people thought he was akin to the Sweet Psalmist of Israel.

Those Israelites had taken their clothes off for their "praise service!" They were dancing in the nude to an African beat, in front of a graven image. These were GOD'S PEOPLE!!! Yes, they were God's people, and they were living like hell-bound sinners! Oh, yes, they were "in the spirit." They no doubt "felt something" in their service. You know, folks today are more interested in finding a church in which they can either "feel comfortable" or "feel the spirit" than they are in finding a church which magnifies the Lord Jesus Christ and preaches the TRUTH.

A lady says, "I love to go to that church because it makes me feel so good! And when I leave there, I can just feel the Lord go with me!" What she means is, the music makes her want to DANCE. She has swayed back and forth to the sound of that worldly music, and she loves it. Listen. When you leave church, you ought to feel motivated to MARCH for the Lord Jesus Christ! Watch out for this music that stirs you to kiss, hug, and dance rather than to get down on your knees and confess your sins!

The devil provides devotional music. The Bible says that in the days of Nebuchadnezzar, when the decree was made for everyone to fall down and worship the golden image the king had set up, the "call to worship" was going to be the playing of musical instruments. What do you think that music sounded like? The Bible doesn't say, but I have an idea it sounded like New Orleans. That's right. Rock and roll had its roots in America in New Orleans, and New Orleans jazz music came from Africa.

This music is **DEVILISH MUSIC**. I'm not just talking about the message. I'm not just talking about the words. I'm talking about the beat and the melody. It is devilish. As I mentioned in the previous chapter, the spirit realm is affected by music even without words. The Bible says that when an evil spirit troubled King Saul, they called for David. The young shepherd boy came with his harp and played before the king, causing the evil spirit to leave Saul. There was no singing, just music being played.

If good music repels evil spirits, it just follows that BAD music will DRAW them. If David played music that made evil spirits leave, I guarantee you there is music that attracts them. The music of "Just As I Am" or "A Mighty Fortress is Our God" would completely change the atmosphere of a honky tonk lounge or a pool hall.

We are dealing with the realm of the supernatural here. Music goes beyond the realm of the natural. God has used music to do supernatural things in the heart. The devil uses HIS music to do supernatural things, as well, only for his only hellish purposes.

CONCLUSION

The end of this chapter brings this book to a close. At this point I want to remind you that the devil is real. He is not natural; he is supernatural. He is powerful, but he is not omnipotent. Only GOD is ALL-powerful. However, Satan should not be under-estimated. May God use this book to help you to recognize him, to resist him, and to "run him off" from you. His work is that of deception, and his great desire is "to be like the most High." Therefore, he imitates the things of God. Be on the alert! What we have covered in this volume is just a sample of **SATAN'S COUNTERFEITS**.

1 John 4:4 Ye are of God, little children, and have overcome them: because greater is he that is in you, than he that is in the world.

1 Peter 5:8 Be sober, be vigilant; because your adversary the devil, as a roaring lion, walketh about, seeking whom he may devour:

www.ingramcontent.com/pod-product-compliance
Lightning Source LLC
Chambersburg PA
CBHW051902090426

42811CB00003B/430